Y0-BRJ-236

STUNTS OF ALL LANDS

STUNTS OF ALL LANDS

By
CATHERINE ATKINSON MILLER
AUTHOR OF "STUNT NIGHT TONIGHT!" "THE SUCCESSFUL YOUNG PEOPLE'S SOCIETY," ETC.

RICHARD R. SMITH, INC.
NEW YORK
1930

PRINTED IN THE UNITED STATES OF AMERICA

For Mother

CONTENTS

Part One

STUNTS!

Part Two

PARTIES!

PART ONE

STUNTS!

I

WHAT MAKES A STUNT SUCCEED?

I

WHAT MAKES A STUNT SUCCEED?

Everyone who plans recreation programs for clubs or schools or churches or even his own family—since there are still families whose members enjoy their good times together—ought to make a large place in those programs for stunts. No other form of recreation offers so many possibilities for sheer, unadulterated fun.

Stunts, indeed, are a revelation of the fun-making powers latent in even the dourest of human beings. Stunts call folk out of their serious shells and show them in all the glory of released imagination, so that the feminine wallflower becomes a sparkling princess and the awkward boy a swash-buckling knight. Bald-headed Mr. Dummer astonishes his fraternal brothers by his flutterings as a Fairy Godmother. Mrs. Peters stops counting calories and counts her steps in a spider-dance which will be the sensation of the meeting of the Tuesday Ladies Club.

Stock market panics may cause hundreds of would-be-travelers to cancel their steamship reservations but stunts will transport you by magic to any country on the globe or on Mars should you prefer to travel beyond the beaten tracks. Since laughter speaks all languages you can enjoy the favorite jokes of every nation when you have made those jokes into stunts and as you laugh *with* other nations you forget how to laugh *at* them. All at once you know that the foreigner and you are not so unlike as you had suspected. All at once you find yourself actually liking him. Then you begin to question just what battleships are good for anyway and you begin to wonder whether the deck of a junked ship wouldn't be a pretty good place to put on some nautical stunts!

Recreation can be a path to world peace and stunts help mightily to make that path.

That being perfectly clear in your mind you are ready to begin to practice what I preach: to plan a stunt night or afternoon or morning. (Why not a Stunt Breakfast?—most of us would look much more attractive in the rotogravure section costumed as gnomes or north winds or terrible Tartars than we look as hunters.) Or, if you have not sufficient time for a whole program of stunts you might include a stunt or two in the party you're giving next month. That would add a touch of novelty to the party and introduce you to stunts if you are still unacquainted.

"But how shall we go about it? How shall we start stunt-ing and where shall we find those funny stories of other lands which will make us laugh ourselves into peace?"

Suppose I try to answer the first part of your

question: to tell you how to start stunt-ing. All that you really need is a group of people. People of any age or size or condition provided they are people whose parents did not forget to invite the fairy-godmother Like-to-Laugh to the christening feast.

For a stunt is a brief dramatization which *may* be quite impromptu and *must* be capable of performance with only one or two rehearsals.

It does not require actors. On the contrary the worse you act the funnier you will be. It may include songs by those who cannot sing and dances by those who were born clumsy and who have grown clumsier every minute. It may make a place for folk who would sooner die than utter a line before an audience by making them parts of the scenery—suns or stars or hat-racks.

The success of stunt staging depends not upon gorgeous costumes, elaborate scenery and lighting but upon the cleverness of your players in taking just any old thing at hand and making it look like something gorgeous. Half the fun of giving stunts is the process of turning sheets and curtains and pajamas and breakfast-food boxes and newspapers into court robes and angel wings and canopied thrones and treasure chests and wild animals. It's the old game of dressing-up-in-the-attic with modern improvements!

I have staged stunts in almost every corner of the continent and have watched group after group of young people develop a new spirit of coöperation in the course of creating stunt plots and contriving costumes. And I have yet to see a Theatre Guild Production which equals in style the stunt given by a group of campers high in the Sierras who had only a suit-case each to call upon for supplies and who performed gallantly even while a forest-fire threatened to shift the scene to "A Heap of Ashes—the Next Morning."

Stunts can be given before an audience. (You can even charge admission and get away with it!) but they are at their best in the company of friends. So your club or your camp or young people's society can be divided into groups and each group allowed a certain amount of time for its stunt. In this case everyone will have a chance to entertain and be entertained and if the continually shifting audience has to appear in at least part of the costumes sooner or later to flash behind the footlights no one will mind at all.

Stunt plots can be found almost everywhere. The very peculiarities of your group may be made into a stunt provided you are very careful not to hurt anyone's feelings. Current events yield innumerable suggestions. Magazine stories, jokes, incidents in history, fairy-tales, folklore, ballads, all will be fruitful once you gain experience in discovering plots. In the following chapters I have given you eleven complete stunts many of which were suggested by folk-lore, since I want you to get acquainted with the folk-tales of other countries. "So This Is Paris!" is modified history. "The Fatal Ride" grew out of a ballad, "The Proud Princess" grew *into* a ballad, and the whole American section is the result of my own lack of inclination to take seriously the "Talkies" and the "Murder Mysteries" and the ladies who win and lose position on the front pages of the newspapers over night. After you have used my samples you will be able to think of dozens of plot-ideas and when you have used *them* you will be as keen to discover new plots as Chief Detective Blackjack is to pick up clues.

Do not overlook the fact that your plot need not be humorous to start with: you may take something appallingly serious in its natural state and by playing it with over-emphasized emotion make it really hilarious. But, please, don't be cheap enough to try to gain a humorous effect by caricaturing really sacred things. As a matter of fact you will lose your sense of what is funny as soon as you lose your appreciation of what is truly fine.

Since stunts are to be presented with little rehearsing the simpler their form the better. That is why I use so many pantomimes with an accompanying reading. For variety you can play behind a lighted sheet, turning your stunt into a shadow-play. Usually, however, an audience appreciates the little details of costume, like the wrist-watch of Menelaus, which do not appear in shadow-plays. Then too, an unusual color effect is always helpful, pink horses, for instance, are so much more distinctive than plain black ones!

Stunts with dialogue may be of several types. An outline of the plot may be read at the beginning of the rehearsal and the players allowed to improvise as they go along. Where the humor depends upon the dialogue careful study is necessary but all stunt parts are short and easily memorized.

In "The Youth and the North Wind" and "The Bored King and the Bandit" a rather new stunt form is used which is effective because of its utter absurdity. The characters say not only the usual speeches but what amounts to the stage directions as well. Played with perfect seriousness this stunt form is amazingly funny.

A stunt stage may be some space at the front of a club-room, a porch, a stretch of lawn at the foot of a hill, with trees for wings and bushes for dressing-room walls, an open pavilion, a cleared place beside a camp-fire or a really truly stage with light switches and everything. The curtain may be absent entirely; it may be indicated by a placarded player who rises and falls; it may be contrived of sheets borne by human curtain poles. Special lighting is unnecessary unless you want to have some fun with spot-lights, in which case, if you are playing out-of-doors, you will find automobile headlights very helpful.

Special scenery is seldom used. The reader may announce the place where the action occurs;

there may be a living program; placards may be used and a few significant properties will convey the desired impression to the audience. Occasionally an impressionistic poster background as in "The Secret of Success" will add so much to the stunt's success that the effort of painting it will be more than justified.

Costumes, as I have already hinted, should be clever make-shifts. I have given you fairly accurate costume descriptions so that your Norwegians won't be mistaken for Japanese and have told you how to make the required costumes but expect that if you are careful to keep to the suggested style you will be able to adapt all sorts of existing costumes at hand, from kimonos to ball-gowns and bathing-suits. As I have explained in "Stunt Night Tonight" it is possible to use just one or two significant items to give the costume idea. The pirate and the minister, for example, might be distinguished only by their head-dress and neck cloths. If all else fail newspapers can always be used as costume material. Crepe paper is versatile and Woolworth jewelry invaluable on Stunt Night. Nor should I neglect to mention those humble but indispensable assistants to the costumer, the safety-pin and the piece of wire.

Cosmetics are used only to exaggerate the natural appearance of the characters so no elaborate make-up box is necessary. There will be plenty of rouge and lip-stick among the regular equipment of your group. You may find that a length of crepe hair will come in handy but you can make whiskers and moustaches of paper and rope and corn-silk and charcoal.

All of the preliminary directions for Stunts are given in fuller form in "Stunt Night Tonight" and I have no desire to write them over again. (It's almost time for dinner and there's good chocolate ice cream. I know because I made it.) But, suppose you are in the middle of the ocean when you read this book and you want to give a stunt immediately? You will need to know how to make heads for animals and birds and there might not be a copy of "Stunt Night Tonight" in the ship's library. So I shall give you a little sample of Stunt Night Tonight! Chapter II.

"Animals are so hard to costume! And birds —impossible!"

Exactly. Impossible birds are just what we want. As for the difficulty of costuming animals——

Here I have made another discovery! Stunt Night audiences really prefer the animal that wears ordinary human dress, provided it has an animal head and tail and possibly some other symbol of its kind—claws for instance.

With slight modification in the way the wires are bent you can create the head of any animal ever known and many never known before. The wire should be stiff enough to hold the shape well: you want ordinary wire at least an eight of an inch in diameter, not silk-covered milliner's wire.

It must, of course, be pliable enough to bend easily.

For the foundation of your animal head take your first wire and make a ring big enough to slip easily over the head of your actor. This ring rests upon his shoulders. Then take a second piece of wire and attach to the ring at one shoulder, carry it up over the head and down to the other shoulder, bending in the shape of the ears. Take a third wire, attach at center front of the ring, carry it up and forward, bending to form shape of nose or snout; catch for firmness in the second wire at the top and carry down to the back of the neck ring. When the wire is very light you may need two third wires. In this case place them a few inches apart. In attaching the wires simply twist them firmly about each other.

Over this wire foundation can be placed an elaborate covering of cloth, but, personally, I prefer one of crepe paper basted into place or merely pinned. Contrasting colored paper is cut out for mouth and eyes and basted or pinned in place. Eyes are improved by being of two colors—a large, light colored eyeball and dark iris—say orange with a black iris. Tiny holes can be cut for sight. A band of paper around the neck after the head is put on will make a neat finish but is not absolutely necessary.

The wire framework, as described, can be used for birds by omitting the ears and making a sharp beak instead of a nose. For insects and worms make the head perfectly round. For dragons, serpents, and other monstrous creatures make it any shape you wish. For a fish's head carry the side wires up to a point and make the wire which goes up the front quite flat. The fish's mouth should be above the top of the human head.

In cases where you do not wish to have the beast or bird appear in human dress you have several alternatives. You may cut the body, hind legs, and fore-paws out of cloth, using a pattern like a child's one-piece sleeping suit, and making mitten-like paws or cutting the paws in one with what would be the arms and legs of the sleeping suit. A quicker way is to baste crepe paper over a suit of pajamas. Dragons may have overlapping paper scales of two colors basted on the pajama foundation.

Now you have shared some of my secrets for making a stunt succeed and you are ready to try some of my new stunts. I hope that they make you as enthusiastic about this form of recreation as I am and that as you laugh at the stunts and play the games which I have brought from other lands you will have a new sense of kinship with all the world.

II

"SEE AMERICA FIRST"

1. *"So This Is Paris!"*
2. *The Blood-Stained Bread Knife*
3. *The Heroine's Husband*

II

1. "SO THIS IS PARIS!"[1]

A "TALKIE" VERSION OF THE ROMANCE OF HELEN OF TROY

CHARACTERS:

The Program
The President of Tantamount Pictures, Ink.
I. M. Scorner, the Director.
The Professor of History.
The Stenographer.
Paris—*A Prince of Troy.*
A Woolly Lamb.
Bo-Peep.
Juno—*Queen of the Gods.*
Athene—*Goddess of Wisdom.*
Venus—*Goddess of Love.*
Priam—*King of Troy.*
Hecuba—*Wife of Priam.*
Cassandra—*Priam's daughter.*
Hector, Helenus } *Priam's sons.*
Menelaus—*King of Sparta.*
Helen—*Daughter of Menelaus.*
Men and women of Troy and Sparta.
Soldiers, etc.

This stunt should contain as many players as possible. It should be a colorful burlesque of the "spectacular" moving pictures.

COSTUMES:

The Program. A short straight tunic of newspaper or of muslin with theatre programs sewn all over it.

The President. Modern suit, very gaudy necktie, flower in buttonhole.

The Director. Soft shirt open at throat, riding breeches and puttees. (Ordinary trousers can be wrapped with bands of tan muslin from ankle to knees.)

The Professor. Long beard, eye-glasses, mussed dark suit.

The Stenographer. Any dress which would be *unsuited* to office wear, elaborately curled hair, too much rouge and lip-stick.

Paris. As a shepherd (and all men not kings). Short bright colored tunic, made of two pieces of dyed unbleached muslin. Cut the material to the correct length (half way between waist and knee at side and few inches longer in front) fasten at shoulders about six inches from the selvedge, girdle tightly at waistline, tack the lower part into pleats. The material beyond the tacked place on shoulders will fall in graceful folds.

Paris as a shepherd wears a cloak—a straight piece of cloth fastened together on one shoulder

—a scoop shaped hat (cut from an old felt hat) and carries a staff.

For the battle scene a corselet of painted black oilcloth or paper is worn over the tunic and a helmet with feathers in cockscomb effect. Shields should be round and decorated with an octopus, or a monkey, or a fish or some strange beast or bird.

Spears may be broomsticks with paper heads, swords cut from heavy cardboard and painted.

Priam, Paris as a Prince, Menelaus. Long robes fastened on shoulder at edge of material. Girdled and bloused at waist. "Walls of Troy" decoration in band around bottom of their robes. This may be painted or basted on. All three have long straight cloaks and band around forehead. Priam and Menelaus wear beards, trimmed to sharp points.

The Shepherdess. Typical "Bo-Peep" costume; full skirt looped up in front over full petticoat. Bodice with high laced girdle, puffed short sleeves. Hair in curls. Black slippers, white stockings. Crook with big bow on the handle.

The Woolly Lamb. Costume may be made like child's one piece sleeping suit with hands and feet covered. If suit is made white flannel should be used. The lamb may wear ordinary white pajamas, white shoes and white gloves. And, of course, a tail.

To make the lamb's head follow the directions for animal heads on page 11.

If preferred make the woolly lamb a black sheep.

The Goddesses and all the Women. Long full robes caught on shoulders like men's short tunics but with longer drapery falling over arms. The robes of the queens hang straight, those of the goddesses and other women are bloused by a girdle. The queens wear cloaks and golden head bands. All the robes should be bright-colored.

Chorus Girls. Dressed in the typical woman's costume.

The Trojan Horse. Body composed of Paris, Priam, Hector and Helenus. Soldiers standing close together with hands on each other's shoulders. Blankets are fastened over them to cover all but head of Paris who is at head of line. He wears a horse's head made according to the directions on page 11.

SCENERY:

The changes of scene are announced by The Program. No special scenery is necessary but suggestive bits will add to the effect, as for instance:

THE PROLOGUE—An office interior—table, desk, typewriter and easy chair or sofa *with pillows.* Pictures of stars.

ACT I. At back of stage hang a poster showing cone shaped mountain against a blue sky, on the mountain print clearly "Mt. Ida." Cover a clothes tree with green paper and have one orange or yellow ball hanging from it.

ACT II. Arrange boards or benches in curving formation around back and right side of stage to indicate a part of a grand-stand. Put an umbrella over the seat of Priam and Hecuba and pillows on the ground beneath it.

ACT III. Arrange a large throne in the background with a low stool beside it. Nothing else is necessary.

ACT IV. Make a very low wall across the stage running diagonally from slightly left of center front to slightly right of center back. The wall may be of compoboard, it may be chairs covered with sheets. In any case see that the "Walls of Troy" design appears on it.

PROLOGUE

The Program appears before the curtain.

Program. Ladies and gentlemen! You are now about to witness the world's most superest superpicture "So This Is Paris!" a triumph of the talking, singing, dancing, fighting, weeping screen. This picture which features one thousand stars in laughs, thrills and sob-stuff, has been one million years in production and cost nine trillion dollars.

This picture features "Eve Adam Herself" as the magnificent Helen of Troy and the part of Paris is played by the World's Best Boy-Friend, Tutti Frutti. You will weep with anguish when you hear Tutti sing his passionate love song "Helen, I'm Tellin'" and thrill at the male chorus of nine hundred and twenty-seven who sing that stirring war-march "Giddiup, my Trojan Horse."

And remember, folks, "So This Is Paris" will be shown at this theatre at only *double* the usual price of admission.

The Program retires then reappears at once to announce—The Office of the President of Tantamount Pictures, Ink.

[*Exeunt Program.*]

The curtain rises.

The President tilts back his chair and dictates rapidly.

The public wants historical romance. In "So This Is Paris" we'll give it to them straight. This picture will be historically accurate. Got that?

Stenographer. Yes, Sir!

Enter Scorner and the Professor shaking their fists violently at each other.

President. What's eating you two?

Professor. This barbarian wants to use a Bo-Peep costume in the first act and the action takes place centuries before that costume was invented!

Scorner. Aw—it's a good costume, who'll know the difference?

President. That's right—and say, I've been reading this here script and it says that Paris runs away with Helen, wife of Menelaus.

Professor. He did!

President. Well, that'll have to be changed. Get this, Miss Keyes—Memo to Scenario Writer——

Stenographer. Yes, Sir!

President. Change Menelaus to father of Helen instead of husband.

Professor. See here, that can't be done! Why! Why!

President. It's got to be done. This here company caters to a nice refined public, our audiences won't stand for any of that triangle stuff. And they want a happy ending so you'll have to make Paris's side win, see?

[*The Professor faints as the curtain falls.*]

Act I

[*Enter Program.*]

Program. This is Act One which takes place on Mount Ida.

The Curtain rises.

[*Paris is seated beneath the tree gazing moodily at nothing. The Shepherdess enters with little skipping steps.*]

Bo-Peep. Ooh—Hoo! Paris! Where's your sheep?

Paris. Oh, hello! Bo-Peep! Haven't you seen him?

Bo-Peep. You're a fine shepherd, you are!

Paris. I'm not really a shepherd, at least I won't be always.

If I Were a Princess
Catherine Atkinson Miller
Moderately
C. Harold Lowden
BO-PEEP
If I were a prin-cess and you were a prince How hap-py we'd both be to-geth-er: We'd dine up-on horse rad-ish, tur-key and quince And laugh at the storm-i-est weth-er.
PARIS
We'd live in a pa-lace of glit-ter-ing gold We'd laugh and we'd love and we'd nev-er grow old.
rit.
I nev-er would fuss! And I
BO-PEEP
nev-er would scold!
BOTH
And we would be hap-py for-ev-er.
PARIS
rit.

Bo-Peep. What will you be?

Paris. A prince!

Bo-Peep. Honest injun?

[*She sings.*]

If I were a princess and you were a prince
How happy we'd both be together!
We'd dine upon horseradish turkey and quince
And laugh at the stormiest weather.

Paris.

We'd live in a palace of glittering gold
We'd laugh and we'd love and we'd never grow old.
I never would fuss!

Bo-Peep. And I never would scold!

Both. We would be happy forever!

[*They dance, after the fashion of a minuet, using stiff little steps. All at once Bo-Peep stops and cries—*]

Bo-Peep. The goddesses are coming and they're cross. I'm scared.

[*The three goddesses enter with a flying motion of their arms. Bo-Peep runs off.*]

The Goddesses. Paris!

Paris. At your service, ladies!

Juno
Athene
Venus } Paris, am I not the most beautiful goddess on Olympus?

[*The lamb enters and nibbles at the tree.*]

Paris. One at a time! Juno, Queen of goddesses, you speak first.

Juno. We want you to give the golden apple to

Give Me the Golden Apple
Catherine Atkinson Miller
Moderately (with expectancy)
C. Harold Lowden
GODDESSES
Give me the gold - en ap - ple,
Choose me, O Pa-ris, Choose now
Give me the gold - en ap - ple,
And you shall be glad, I vow,
JUNO
I'll give you wealth and pow - er.
If you will on - ly choose me,

ATHENE
Wis-dom will be your dow - er If
you my charms can see.
VENUS
I'll give you
joy un-meas-ured,
I'll make you hap-py for
life
Give me the gold - en ap -
ple,
Just for a beau-ti - ful wife.

the one who is most beautiful. If you say I am I'll give you wealth and kingly power.

The Lamb. Blah! Blah!

Athene. I, Athene, will make you wise! I'll make you a hero!

The Lamb. Blah! Blah!

Venus. I, Venus, will give you the most beautiful wife in the world.

The Lamb. Blah!

Paris. Dear me! What shall I do? You are all so beautiful!

The Lamb. Apple-sauce!

The Goddesses [*Singing*].

Give me the golden apple,
Choose me, oh Paris, choose now.
Give me the golden apple,
You shall be glad, I vow.

Juno.

I'll give you wealth and power,
If you will only choose me.

Athene.

Wisdom will be your dower
If you my charms can see.

Venus.

I'll give you joy unmeasured
I'll make you happy for life
Give me the golden apple
Just for a beautiful wife.

[*They dance in a ring around Paris, then Paris takes the hand of each in turn, swings her around, bows, passes to the next goddess. He plucks the orange from the tree and holds it until the chorus ends. There is a moment of silence, then Paris kneels and hands the apple to Venus.*]

Juno. Wretch!

Athene. Villain!

[*They go off angrily.*]

Venus. Paris, return to Troy, your home. There claim the honor due you as a prince. There wait until I send you forth to win your beautiful bride.

Paris. I will obey!

[*Venus goes out, sucking the orange. Bo-Peep skips in.*]

Paris. A prince! A beautiful bride!
Good-bye, Bo-Peep, you've been a good pal.

Bo-Peep. Oh Paris, don't leave me.

Paris. I must. It is my Fate.

[*He goes out. Bo-Peep puts her arm around the Lamb and sings.*]

If I were a princess and you were a prince
How happy we'd both be together.

[*She sobs and buries her face in the Lamb's wool as*]

The curtain falls.

Act II

[*Enter Program.*]

Program. This is act two which takes place in the great amphitheatre of Troy.

The curtain rises.

[*Enter Cassandra, Hector and Helenus. Cassandra always speaks in a slow mournful voice (like Zazu Pitts) and never smiles.*]

Cassandra. I'm *sure* it's going to rain.

Hector. Oh, Cassandra you're always looking for trouble.

Helenus. Look on the shiny side of life, Cassie. Turn your dark clouds inside out and look for a blue bird!

[*He sings.*]

Don't chase trouble!
Trouble comes to everybody
Just smile double
And trouble will pass by!
Don't be a quitter
Smile and hear the blue birds twitter
Don't chase trouble!
For sunny days are nigh.

[*All three dance as they repeat, "Don't Chase Trouble." The dance should be a fantastic imitation of a tap dance and end with all three sitting down hard on the grandstand, looking at the sky, then smiling in relief.*]

[*Enter a Trojan boy in short tunic.*]

Don't Chase Trouble

Boy. Peanuts! Pop corn! Soda water! Hot dogs!

Cassandra. I want some peanuts.

[*She buys a bag using a modern dollar bill.*]

[*Enter Priam, Hecuba, other Trojans. When all are seated a Trojan with a sweater over his tunic comes to the front and announces.*]

Umpire. I am the umpire. The first event, ladies and gents will be the discus throw.

[*Hector and Helenus scramble out of their seats and go to the left side of the stage. The umpire hands each one a paper plate. They throw in turn.*]

Crowd. Rotten! Kill the umpire!

Umpire. Any other hero wanta try?

[*Enter Paris.*]

Paris. Give me a shot!

[*He makes a long throw. Everyone yells and claps. Paris bows to the audience.*]

Cassandra. I want a bottle of pop.

[*There is confusion until the boy is summoned and she gets the drink.*]

Umpire. The next event is the shot put.

[*Hector, Helenus and Paris throw blown-up paper bags. Paris wins. The audience, including the king and queen rushes down off the stand and thumps him on the back.*]

Priam. Who are you, hero?

Paris. I am your long lost son, Paris!

Cassandra. Oh dear! Now there'll be three brothers to eat the chocolates my beaux bring me.

Hecuba. Heat up the hash! We'll feast in state this day!

[*Everyone—singing—Don't chase trouble, etc.*]

[*They march around in lockstep with Paris leading and go off, still singing.*]

ACT III

[*Enter the Program.*]

Program. This is the famous third act in which Tutti Frutti, as Prince Paris elopes with Eve Adam Herself in the part of Helen. From this act on the plot of this super-film will be a great improvement over the story the way Homer wrote it. Tantamount Pictures Company Ink can improve any story.

[*Exeunt Program.*]

[*The curtain rises upon the Court of Sparta. Menelaus is seated upon his throne. At his side on a low stool sits Helen. Here you have a chance to use your imagination by beginning the scene with a special feature which would be likely to entertain the king. I use a chorus of dancers (preferably girls who can't dance!) who do a clumsy classic dance chasing huge paper butterflies which they themselves dangle on wires. When the dance ends the dancers stand at the sides of the stage.*]

Helen [*Yawning*]. Nothing ever happens in this pokey place.

[*Enter a servant. He kneels before the King.*]

Servant. Your Majesty, Prince Paris of Troy is without.

Menelaus. Without what?

Helen. The key of the city, I guess, Daddy. You remember Ulysses forgot to give it back when he left after his visit here last Monday. Or did we lend it to Cleopatra that time she had company from Rome?

Menelaus. Show Prince Paris right in. Tell him this city is so honest we don't need locks and keys.

[*Exeunt the Servant.*]

[*Enter Paris and Venus. They stop at the doorway.*]

Venus. There she is! Now remember, only the brave deserve the fair! Be brave.

[*Exeunt Venus.*] [*Paris bows before Menelaus.*]

Paris. Oh King, I have come to beg the hand of your daughter, the fair Princess Helen, in marriage.

Menelaus. I never give to beggars. It is against my principles. Present this card at the office of the organized charities.

Helen. Oh, Daddy, I like this young man.

Menelaus. You may talk with him for three minutes while I speak to the prime minister about affairs of state.

[*He looks at his wrist-watch.*]

[*Exeunt Menelaus.*] [*Paris kneels before Helen.*]

Paris. Now is our chance, Beautiful! We must elope before he returns.

Helen. But how do I know you *really* love me?

Paris [*Singing with passionate ardor*].

Helen, I'm tellin'
My deathless love for you
To ever flow-wer
And every sky so blue.
Each little hou-er
Without you dear, seems sad,
Unless you'll wed me
I know that I will just go mad
For Helen, I'm tellin'
The secret of my heart
Helen, I'm tellin'
You, we must not part.

Helen [*Throwing herself in his arms*]. My hero!

[*They hurry out, bumping into Menelaus in the doorway as he returns.*]

Menelaus. Bother! Now I'll have to start another war!

[*Curtain.*]

Act IV

[*Enter the Program.*]

Program. This, you will be sorry to hear is the last act. But it has a happy ending!

The action takes place just outside of the walls of Troy. King Menelaus's army has won so far. They have recaptured Helen and tomorrow they

Helen I'm Tellin'
Catherine Atkinson Miller
C. Harold Lowden
Ardently
Hel-en, I'm tell-in' My death-less love for you
To ev-'ry flow-wer and ev-'ry sky so blue, Each lit-tle
hou-er with-out you dear, seems sad. Un-less you'll wed me I
know that I will just go mad For Hel-en, I'm tell-in' The se-cret of my
heart. Hel-en, I'm tell-in' you We must not part.

will take her home—unless something happens to stop them.

[*Exeunt Program.*]

[*The curtain rises. The light is very dim. Paris is standing on a box looking over the wall. On the other side—supposedly outside of the city—is Cassandra. Her hair is tightly knotted at the back and she wears a false beard.*]

Paris. Hist!

Cassandra. I'm histing.

[*She produces a spy-glass and looks all around. Then whispers*—]

The Army of Sparta will return any minute. Menelaus just went out to look for a new horse.

Paris. A horse! That gives me an idea. I may yet recover my lovely bride.

[*He sings—"Helen, I'm tellin'," etc.*]

Cassandra. What's the idea?

[*Paris leans over and whispers then jumps down behind the wall just as Menelaus and his army—all three of them—enter with Helen bound in chains.*]

Menelaus. You'll not escape again, my girl. As soon as I can buy a horse we shall be off for Sparta.

Helen [*Weeping*]. Oh! Oh! Oh! Oh!

Menelaus. "A horse! A horse! My kingdom for a horse!"

Cassandra. Do you want a good horse, mister! Will you take it an' no questions asked?

Menelaus. Not a question.

Gallop On, Trojan Horse
Catherine Atkinson Miller
C. Harold Lowden
Quickly
CASSANDRA
A dar - ing deed is to be done Be-
fore the light of dawn, A dar - ing bat - tle's
to be won Be - fore the night is gone The
fate of Troy de - pends on you True lov - er's joy de-

pends on you So to your du-ty now be true My Tro-jan Horse!
MENS VOICES
Gid - di - up! Tro - jan Horse! Through the
night gal - lop on! In your might gal - lop on! To the
fight gal - lop on! For the right gal - lop on, Gal - lop
on, gal-lop on, gal-lop on, gal-lop on, gal-lop on, Tro-jan Horse!

Cassandra. Give me three thousand dollars and meet me here at midnight to-night.

Menelaus [*Giving the money*]. 'Tis a bargain.

[*The curtain falls but rises again at once. The Spartans are sleeping upon the ground. The Trojan horse enters on the Trojan side of the wall led by Cassandra. It stalks around a few times and Cassandra sing*]—

Cassandra.

A daring deed is to be done
Before the light of dawn
A daring battle's to be won
Before the night is gone
The fate of Troy depends on you
True lover's joy depends on you
So to your duty now be true
My Trojan horse.

Chorus [*In which the horse joins*].

Giddiup! Trojan Horse
Through the night gallop on
In your might gallop on
To the fight gallop on
For the right gallop on
Gallop on, gallop on, gallop on, gallop on!
Trojan Horse!

[*The horse, led by Cassandra climbs the wall and stands behind the sleeping Spartans.*]

Cassandra. Here's your horse, mister King!

[*Menelaus and his men rise sleepily. Helen gets up and pats the horse as best she can with her hands chained. Suddenly, with a great cry Paris throws off the horse's head. Hector, Helenus and Priam throw off the covering blankets and kill the Spartans. Paris clasps Helen in his arms. All the other players rush in. Priam embraces Hecuba, the Peanut Boy embraces Venus, Hector takes Juno, Helenus Athene, the Umpire Cassandra and all sing as the grand finale—"If I were a princess and you were a prince."*]

[*Curtain.*]

2. THE BLOOD-STAINED BREAD KNIFE

A THRILLING MYSTERY STUNT

CHARACTERS:

Fullo Bunk—*The World's greatest authority on the mental processes of canary birds.*
Chief Detective Blackjack.
Professor Mush.
Alotta Mush—*His daughter.*
Mike—*A policeman.*
Ike—*A finger print expert.*
The Veiled Woman.
The Prince of Roccoco.
Sonny Boy.
The Butler.
The Cook.

The setting for The Blood-Stained Bread Knife should suggest a living-room. The furniture may be simple or elaborate as you prefer but should include a table near the center-front and a high-backed chair placed diagonally at left-rear. There should be a screen across the corner at right-rear and a box at right-front to give the effect of a small safe. On the center-table stands a telephone —preferably not a real one. To create the telephone illusion use a tin funnel fastened to a Five and Ten Cent Store hat stand with a large empty spool for a receiver. Or invent your own variety!

COSTUMES:

Fullo Bunk. Wears an ordinary dark suit or white trousers and a dark coat. He must look ultra sleek and shiny. He may have a high hat and he must have a flower in his buttonhole.

Sergeant Blackjack. Wears a dark suit and has a variety of false beards and mustaches in his pocket and a police officer's badge on his vest. He should show a particular fondness for chewing dill pickles and should always be seen nibbling at said pickle so that the audience will recognize him even if the villain is fooled by his disguise.

Professor Mush. Looks just the way you expect him to look, a bit shabby and absent-minded and characterized by spectacles and a flowing tie.

Alotta Mush. A sweet young thing in blue and white.

Mike. Policeman's uniform.

Ike. Ordinary clothes and a derby hat if available.

The Veiled Woman. All black, of course, and a long black veil draped over her head, no hat.

The Prince of Roccoco. Ordinary clothes and a Hindoo turban. Bath towels make excellent turbans with bead necklaces looped across them.

Sonny Boy. Large for his age (very large) but dressed in knickers or shorts, a white blouse and big tie. He carries a large doll or Teddy Bear or Calico Cat.

The Butler. Cutaway coat, high collar, dark trousers, whiskers.

The Cook. Your audience will expect her to be big and buxom and to arrive wearing a little bonnet or small hat perched high on a top-knot, a shawl and a skirt that is very full. She should have a suitcase, an umbrella, and a cat.

[*The curtain rises discovering Alotta Mush at the telephone, her face turned directly toward the audience.*]

Allotta [*Desperately*]. Hello! Hello! I want a fire-engine! No, I mean a policeman! Hello! Police Headquarters? Send your best detective to 1234 Front Street at once. Yes. What? This is the home of Professor Aloysius Mush. This is Alotta Mush speaking. Yes! Yes! Hurry! It is a case of life or death! Which? I don't know which that's why I want a detective, to find out. Yes! Hurry!

[*She replaces the receiver as the Professor enters.*]

The Professor. Have you seen my spectacles?

Alotta. Yes, Father Darling, they are on your nose.

Professor. Oh, thank you, thank you, my child. And now, when can we expect the detectives to clean up this dreadful mystery?

[*A bell rings. The Butler ushers in Fullo Bunk and Blackjack.*]

Butler. The persons from the Stockyards, Sir!

Bunk. My good man, I am *not* a person.

Blackjack. Certainly not! This here gent is the famous Mr. Fullo Bunk himself. I just happened to be having tea and muffins with him when your call came so I brought him along. He's the greatest amachure detective in the world.

[*Bunk bows.*]

Blackjack. Now then, where's the body. The first step is to mark x where the body lay.

[*He takes out a huge piece of chalk.*]

Professor. [*After a fearsome look around.*] There-is-no-body!

Bunk. Ah, I felt it! This is a curiously involved case!

Blackjack. But how do you know *who* was murdered?

Alotta [*In a terrible whisper*]. We don't *know* who was murdered!

Bunk. This is no ordin'ry case!

Blackjack blows a whistle and Mike and Ike enter. Ike carries a large box.

Blackjack. Officer Mike, guard both front and rear of this house. Allow no one to enter or leave.

[*Mike salutes and goes out.*]

[*Fingerprint and Caliber of Revolver Expert Ike, remain here ready for duty.*]

Ike. Ready, Chief.

Bunk. With your permission, Professor, let us sit down quietly and discuss this extraordin'ry case.

[*All sit.*]

Now then, Professor, who discovered the crime?

Alotta. I did. I went into the kitchen to make fudge—it's cook's day out—and when I opened the drawer of the kitchen cabinet to get a spoon I saw it. [*She shudders.*]

Blackjack
Bunk } What?
Ike

Alotta. A blood-stained bread knife!

[*As she says the words the head of Prince Roccoco appears above the chair in which Bunk is sitting. He glares around with terrible hatred then disappears. He could easily be seen by Alotta or Blackjack who are facing him but Alotta is powdering her nose and Blackjack is busy nibbling at his pickle.*]

Blackjack. Where is this knife?

Alotta. In the kitchen, Sir. I was afraid to touch it. Shall I have it brought in?

Blackjack. At once.

[*Alotta rings a hand bell and the Butler brings in the knife on a large tray. He holds it as far from him as possible. Ike at once shakes powder—from a flour shaker—on the knife and peers at it through a magnifying glass. He gives a startled cry.*]

Ike. Ah!

Blackjack. Whose finger-prints are they?

Ike. The finger-prints of the Prince of Roccoco!

[*At the words, the Prince's head appears again for a moment, glares and disappears.*]

Bunk. Ah, the Prince is now touring this country in search of the pink emerald stolen from the head of the Goddess. The Prince could have been in this house for but one reason.

All. What?

Bunk. Villainy!

[*They all shudder. Suddenly Alotta screams.*]

Alotta. Sonny Boy! Sonny Boy hasn't appeared and school has been out an hour. Sonny Boy has been killed!

[*The head of the Veiled Woman appears for a moment above the screen. It is shaken sadly then disappears.*]

Bunk. Search the cellar and the attic while I interview the servants!

[*Blackjack puts on a false moustache.*]

[*All go out but Bunk, and, of course, the Prince and the Veiled Lady. Bunk takes a ribbon-tied box from his pocket, opens it, chooses a chocolate with great care, reties the box, returns it to his pocket. He nibbles thoughtfully as the Butler enters.*]

Butler. You sent for me, Sir!

Bunk. You were in the house all afternoon?

Butler. Yes, Sir!

Bunk. Did you observe anything, ah, suspicious?

Butler. Yes, Sir!

Bunk. Report precisely what you observed.

Butler. I saw Professor Mush take out a pink emerald and polish it carefully.

Bunk. Ah! You saw no signs of a corpse?

Butler. No, Sir! But I will say that a blood-stained bread knife looks mighty serious, Sir!

Bunk. Where does the Professor keep the pink emerald?

[*The head of the Prince and the Veiled Lady both rise quickly at this. They watch intently as the Butler shows Bunk the safe. They do not see each other.*]

Butler. Here Sir, in this concealed safe.

Bunk. Thank you, my man. Now if you'll show me the kitchen cabinet.

[*They go out. Instantly the Prince comes from behind the chair, the Veiled Lady from behind the Screen. They rush toward the safe, bump into each other and stop.*]

The Prince. Out of my way, minion!

[*She falls back and he opens the safe, quickly takes the jewel and goes out. She follows him. When they have gone, Bunk, the Butler, Blackjack, Ike, the Professor and Alotta return. Alotta sees the open safe.*]

Alotta. Father Darling, my dowry has been stolen.

Professor [*Sinking into a chair*]. It is gone!

Mike [*Entering with the Prince clutched with one hand, the Veiled Lady with the other*]. Here's the rascals, Sir.

Bunk. Ah, the Prince of Roccoco. Where have you hid the corpse?

Prince [*On his knees*]. I am innocent, I swear it! I am here only to recover the pink emerald, stolen from the head of the goddess by Professor Mush.

Bunk. Did you do this, Professor?

Professor [*Hanging his head*]. It *was* naughty of me but I liked the color so much! And I had no dowry for my daughter.

Bunk [*Gallantly*]. She needs none!

Alotta. Oh, Sir!

Blackjack. Who is this woman? And how did this Prince guy's finger-prints get on the bread knife.

Prince. I can explain! I was going to use it to jimmy open the safe but when I picked it up I saw blood and dropped it.

Bunk. The feller seems to be tellin' the truth, don't y' know!

Blackjack. Then who killed——

Alotta. Sonny Boy! Our little Sonny Boy! Oh! Oh!

[*At this point Sonny Boy enters.*]

Sonny Boy [*In high, piping voice*]. Is this a party, Sister Dear?

Alotta [*Seizing him in her arms*]. Darling! Where have you been?

Sonny Boy. I got kept in after school. I'm *so* ashamed.

[*He sobs.*]

Ike. Then who killed——?

Blackjack. Who was killed?

Bunk. This is a most confusin' case.

Professor. Who is that woman?

The Veiled Lady [*Throwing back her veil*]. I am the Princess of Roccoco. I knew my husband had set out upon a dangerous enterprise. I followed him, to die with him if need be.

Prince [*Catching her in his arms*]. Beloved! Can I ever repay such devotion? Come, let us go back to our palace in triumph. We have recovered the pink emerald.

[*He glares at the others, embraces the lady and they go out.*]

Blackjack. But we still have the Blood-stained Bread Knife.

[*Enter the Cook.*]

Cook. Sure and a little Dutch cleanser will clean it. 'Tis but a bit of blood from the liver I was slicin' for me cat. I had to use the bread knife since the carvin' knife was on the lunch-table with the roast. An' be like, in me hurry to see the beginnin' of Doria Glonson's picture I neglected to wipe it off, at all!

[*The others look very sleepish as the curtain quickly falls.*]

3. THE HEROINE'S HUSBAND

CHARACTERS:

The Heroine.
The Mayor.
A Bellboy.
The Manager of the Hotel.
The Moving Picture Magnate.
Reporters.
The Husband.

The scene is a room in a hotel with a window overlooking Fifth Avenue, New York. It is a very luxurious room, luxury being typified by numerous fluffy pillows and bunches of flowers. The flowers, of course, should be huge and obviously artificial. They might even be made of newspaper.

The curtain rises to show the Heroine, in aviator's costume, powdering her nose at a mirror. The Husband, hands deep in pockets strides up and down the room.

The Heroine. Darling, do be quiet. I must be quite calm when the reception committee arrives. They will be *so* disappointed about failing to meet me at the dock.

The Husband. Committees! Committees! What

about me! Have I no rights? Just because you flew from Boston to New York.

The Heroine. Darling, I do believe you're jealous.

[*A knock at the door.*]

Come in!

[*A bell-boy enters with an armload of flowers.*]

Oh, how lovely! John, do tip this nice boy for his trouble!

[*John ungraciously finds a tip.*]

The Husband. I'm sick and tired of mending my own socks. Are you coming home with me or not. After all, woman's place is——

The Heroine. Darling, you're *so* old fashioned!

[*A knock at the door.*]

Come in!

[*Enter the Hotel Manager.*]

Manager. Are you quite comfortable, madame? It is an honor to have such a heroine for our guest. There will be no bill for madame.

The Husband. Say, I guess I can pay my wife's bills.

The Heroine. Darling! [*To the Manager.*] The room is just lovely and you're *so* kind.

[*She smiles sweetly as he goes out, then—*]

John! Will you please try not to act like a mere milkman?

The Husband. I'm proud to be a milkman and you should be proud to be my wife.

The Heroine [*Amused*]. *Darling!* My career——

[*A knock at the door. At the Heroine's gracious "Do come in" enter the Mayor, the Reporters, the Movie Magnate.*]

A Reporter. Will you give me your own story? Will you keep on flying or will you sacrifice your career for your home and fireside? Will you——

The Mayor [*Interrupting*]. Madame, it is my high privilege to present to you the Key to the City.

The Heroine. Oh, how lovely! [*She puts it on the table.*]

The Husband. I just want to say——

The Movie Magnate. Madame, will you accept a contract to star for two years at one thousand dollars a week? [*She places it on the table.*]

The Heroine. Oh, how lovely.

The Husband. Now, look here, this has gone far enough. My wife——

Bellboy [*Interrupting*]. More flowers for madame!

The Heroine. Lovely!

Reporter. Now, about that story, do you believe——

[*There is a great shouting outside—all rush to the window, pushing the Heroine and the Husband out of the way.*]

The Mayor. What are they crying?

A Reporter. They're cheering Maizie Daisey. She's just returned from flying from Boston to Philadelphia without once stopping to powder her nose!

The Heroine [*Crushed by the blow of fate, sinking into a chair*]. Ah!

The Mayor [*Picking up the Key to the City*]. I'm sorry but we'll need this right away.

[*He goes out hurriedly.*]

The Heroine. Oh!

The Movie Magnate [*Picking up the contract*]. Since you haven't signed this——

[*He rushes after the Mayor.*]

The Heroine. Oh! Oh!

[*The Hotel Manager enters.*]

Manager. Madame, I regret that we shall need this room at once.

The Heroine. Oh, Oh, Oh!

The Husband. It is too small. Reserve your best suite for us for the week.

Manager [*Surprised*]. Of course, Sir!

[*He goes out.*]

The Heroine [*Rapturously*]. Darling!

The Husband [*Firmly catching the last escaping reporter by the collar*]. Take my wife's story.

[*The Reporter hesitates but the Husband looks grim. The Reporter prepares to write.*]

The Heroine [*Putting her arm about her Husband's shoulders and pressing her cheek against his*]. Just say that I'm prouder of being the wife of a milkman than of any heroic flight I could make. Say that I believe that——

The Reporter. You believe that——

The Heroine. Woman's place is in the home!

[*Curtain.*]

III

ONE ARABIAN NIGHT WAS STUNT NIGHT

The Secret of Success

III

ONE ARABIAN NIGHT WAS STUNT NIGHT

THE SECRET OF SUCCESS*

CHARACTERS:

The Teacher.
Ali Ben Bey.
The Grand Vizier.
Palace Guards.
The Caliph.
The Caliph's Daughter.
Two Troubled Fish.
The King Fish.
Slaves.

COSTUMES:

All the men except the guards and slaves wear long robes girdled at the waist. All wear turbans. The teacher's is dark and tightly bound to his head, and a long shawl is worn over his turban. Ali has a very small turban or a cap the shape of a round box about four inches high. The Grand

* Adapted from the poem "Preserve and Prosper" by John Godfrey Saxe.

Vizier has a gayly colored turban, the Caliph's turban is purple and covered with jewels. Ali has a short sleeveless jacket over his coat, the Grand Vizier has a sleeveless coat to his knees and that of the Caliph is as long as his gown and gorgeously colored.

The palace guards wear short tunics which cover one shoulder and leave the other shoulder bare. They have huge swords with curved blades which they hold with both hands resting on the hilt and the top on the ground in front of them. The slaves wear straight tunics and small turbans.

The Caliph's daughter wears a long gown, girdled at the hips and has her head and face covered with a veil so that only her eyes appear.

Since only the heads of the fish appear they need only wire and paper heads. See page 11. Make the heads of the very vivid colors with large eyes. Put a tiny golden crown on the head of the King Fish.

Scenery:

This stunt can be played without special scenery but will be "absolutely wonderful" played before a background like the illustration. This may be painted on compoboard, muslin or even paper and the whole fastened upon screens. The doorway to the Vizier's Palace should be cut out and a curtain may be hung behind it to conceal the interior of the Palace.

The palm tree at the left should be separate

The line A-B is the bottom of the poster, resting on the floor. The palm tree, which looks like a banana split, is cut separately.

and set out about two feet from the rest of the scenery so that the fishes' heads, popping out from behind it, will seem to be rising out of the river. Color the palace salmon pink, the river and sky bright blue, the tree trunks brown and the grass and bushes green. Make all the outlines of black to give a poster effect to the whole.

PART ONE

[*The curtain rises discovering the Teacher and Ali seated cross-legged in front of the bush. The Palace guards stand silently at each side of the Palace door.*]

Teacher.

Now please remember, my dear,
You are sure to win whatever you plan
If you steadily persevere.

Ali.

Well, I'm going to try this very day
If you've taught me what is true.

Teacher.

My teaching is honest, but tell if you can
Just what you are planning to do.

Ali.

I mean to try, tho' it cost my life
'Though I go through fire and water,
Since every man wishes to marry a wife—
I'll marry the Caliph's daughter!

[*The Teacher raises his hands in horror as the curtain falls.*]

Part Two

[*The Grand Vizier stands in the Palace doorway, Ali kneels before him. The guards stand as before.*]

Grand Vizier.

Now, after your earnest daily pleading,
I come to hear what you are needing.
Has injustice been your lot?
Do you seek to serve the Caliph? Or what?

Ali.

Hear me now, my Lord Vizier—[*Veesyer*].
While *you're* judge injustice can't occur!
I come not to complain but to plead instead
That the Caliph's daughter I may wed!

Grand Vizier.

Guards! Remove this silly lad!
Such impudence! You must be mad!

[*The guards push Ali away but he comes back.*]

Ali.

You will not heed my plea. All right,
I'll kneel at your door here day and night,
Always before you I shall be
Until you grant that I may see
The Caliph, and make to him my plea.

Grand Vizier.

Kneel then! Until your knees wear out.
You're raving mad beyond a doubt!

[*He goes into the Palace leaving Ali kneeling before the door.*]

PART THREE

[*The guards as before. 'Ali still kneeling. The Caliph enters at the left preceded by slaves. His daughter walks beside him. As the Caliph approaches the Palace the Grand Vizier comes out and bows to the ground. 'Ali stares at the Caliph without bowing.*]

Caliph.

How now! What means this insolence
Bow, lad! Or take the consequence!

[*The guards raise their swords.*]

Grand Vizier.

Your majesty, this case is sad,
This comely lad is raving mad.

The Princess.

He's very handsome. It *is* sad.

'Ali.

Your Majesty, mad I am not
But I have vowed that on this spot
I'll kneel until you hear my plea.

Caliph.

Make known your wishes unto me!

'Ali.

My wish is very quickly said:
Your lovely daughter I would wed.

Caliph.

Now by my venerable head,
'Tis only the wise and great
A Caliph's daughter may ask to wed,
For rank with rank must mate,

Unless, mayhap, some valiant deed
May serve for equal claim
For merit, I own, should have its meed
And princes yield to fame.

'Ali.

Whatever the task you set for me
I vow it will accomplished be.

Princess.

He's as brave as comely, I begin
To hope this lad my hand may win.

Caliph.

In the Tigris once a gem was lost,
'Twas ages and ages since.
A ruby of wondrous size and cost
And fit for the noblest prince.
That gem, my lad, must surely be
Somewhere beneath the water.
Go, find it, boy, and bring it to me,
Then come and marry my daughter!

'Ali [*Jumping up*].

Your Majesty, I'll find the stone
And claim the Princess for my own.

[*The curtain falls.*]

Part Four

[*The guards as usual. 'Ali is kneeling on his left knee, facing toward the large bush, dipping water out of the river with a little cup. (The water is in a bowl behind the bush.) The two troubled fishes' heads appear.*]

First Fish.
And still with his cup he dips away!
Now what is the fellow about?

Second Fish.
If he keeps on dipping night and day
He'll drain the Tigris out.

First Fish.
This matter must come before our king,
It is a very dreadful thing!

[*The Troubled Fishes' heads disappear. Immediately afterward the King Fish's head appears.*]

King Fish.
Now why are you dipping our river away,
And what do you please to wish—
If you keep on dipping night and day,
We'll all soon be dead fish.

Ali.
Good fish, I want the ruby red,
That's hidden in the river bed.

King Fish.
Well, please to let us alone,
Stop your dipping and go away
And the ruby shall be your own.

Ali.
I promise, oh very noble fish!

[*King Fish disappears, immediately returning and dropping the stone from his mouth to Ali's hand.*]

King Fish.
Then go, for here is what you wish!

[*Ali jumps up and shouts.*]

Ali.

Victory! I've won from out the water!
The stone of wondrous size.

[*The Caliph, preceded by the slaves, followed by the Grand Vizier and the Princess comes out of the Palace door. The Caliph takes the ruby and examines it carefully.*]

Caliph.

So perseverance wins the prize
And you may have my daughter!

[*Ali and the Princess embrace as the curtain falls.*]

IV

JOLLY STUNTS FROM GERMANY

1. *The Fatal Ride.*
2. *The Proud Princess*

IV

1. THE FATAL RIDE*

CHARACTERS:

The Lady Eleanora von Alleyne.
A lady in waiting.
Knights.
The Margrave Gondibert.
The Jester.

COSTUMES:

The Lady Eleanora wears a long full gown with a tightly fitted waist and long, tight sleeves. The neck is cut in a wide V, low on each shoulder and in the front. She wears a tall, cone-shaped head-dress with a long scarf fastened to the point, and flowing down her back. She has many jewels.

The Lady in Waiting wears a plain dress of the same type as Lady Eleanor's but with the waist open down the front and laced over a white vest. Instead of the high head-dress she has a white head-dress of muslin fitted tightly across the top of her head and under her chin and extending in points several inches from each ear.

* Adapted from *The Ride Round the Parapet* by Friedrich Rueckert, translated by James Clarence Mangan.

The Knights are in armor, of course. It can be made of gray cambric or oilcloth or even stiff brown paper.

The horses should be cut from card-board, with one front leg and one back leg, a long paper mane and bushy paper tail. They can be colored according to the fancy of each knight. Pink horses are lovely, so are pale blue or green ones.

Each horse should have a loop of tape fastened to the middle of its back. When the knights dismount to greet Lady Eleanora they may hang the loop on a tack in the castle wall and give the effect of the horse standing alone. This little trick is worth the price of admission all by itself.

The Jester. The usual pointed tunic with a bell on each point, pointed cowl with bells on the point.

SCENERY:

Scenes I and III The Lady Eleanora's Castle.

Gray castle walls indicated by curtains, gray blankets, paper covered screens or painted compoboard. An opening in the walls to indicate the entrance into the castle-yard. If you are very clever you may contrive a draw-bridge to be lowered for the entrance of each knight. The tower and parapet are contrived by making a circle of chairs with seats turned out, covering the seats, placing a compoboard tower to hide the backs and another strip of compoboard from the floor to a few inches above the seats. Cut the top of this strip to indicate the unevenly laid stones . . . Naturally the humorous effect of the dangerous ride depends in large measure upon the fact that it is really a *very low* parapet!

The highway at Gratz is indicated merely by closing the stage curtains and having the Margrave and his friend meet in front of the curtains. He can train his horse there also.

ACTION:

The stunt is a pantomime accompanied by the reading of the ballad by the Jester.

The Jester announces "The Fatal Ride—Part One." The Courtyard of the Lady Eleanora's Castle.

The action follows the reading very closely. The curtain rises discovering Lady Eleanora talking to her lady-in-waiting. The Jester reads the first stanza. During the first two lines of the second stanza a knight arrives, dismounts, hangs his horse from a tack in the castle wall, bows before the Lady and mounts as the Jester reads the third line. He rides and falls as the stanza is concluded. All the knights should ride slowly and carefully, giving an exaggerated emphasis to the great danger of the ride.

The same action accompanies the third stanza, with the fourth the action must be quicker. At least three knights must ride to represent the "six and thirty."

The curtain falls at the end of this stanza.

The Jester announces, "*Part Two—the Highway to Gratz.*"

The Margrave Gondibert rides out from the left, another knight from the right. They salute, dismount and talk. The Jester reads stanza one of Part Two.

The other knight mounts, rides away and the Jester reads stanza two. The Margrave places some stones and rides his horse around them, then rides off.

The Jester announces—"*Part Three, the Courtyard of the Lady Eleanora's Castle*" and reads stanza one of Part Three as the Margrave gallops in and greets Lady Eleanora. She expresses delight in the meeting but looks terrified as the Jester reads stanza two and the Margrave mounts and rides up on the parapet. During the reading of stanzas three and four the Margrave rides faster and faster and the Lady violently expresses her emotion. She may squeeze tears from a wet sponge or drop paper ones. She must shake wildly and the burning fire in her bosom may be shown by a small flashlight concealed beneath her dress.

While the Jester reads stanza five the Margrave rides off and dismounts. The Lady runs to him and claps her hands with glee. During stanza six she tells with gestures that he is to wed her. During seven the Margrave bows and replies with much scorn. As the stanza ends the Lady falls in a faint and he mounts and rides away.

The Jester [*Reading*]. The Fatal Ride.

PART ONE

The Courtyard of the Lady Eleanora's Castle

"My feeling towards Man is one of utter scornfulness,"
Said Lady Eleanora von Alleyne.
"My feeling towards Man is one of utter scornfulness,
And he that would o'ercome it, let him ride around the summit
Of my battlemented Castle by the Maine,"
Said the Lady Eleanora,
Said the Lady Eleanora von Alleyne.

So came a knight anon to ride around the parapet,
For Lady Eleanora von Alleyne,
So came a knight anon to ride around the parapet.
Man and horse were hurled together o'er the crags that beetled nether.
Said the Lady, "There, I fancy, they'll remain!"
Said the Lady Eleanora,
Queenly Lady Eleanora von Alleyne!

Then came another knight to ride around the parapet,
For Lady Eleanora von Alleyne.
Then came another knight to ride around the parapet,

Man and horse fell down, asunder, o'er the crags
that beetled under.
Said the Lady, "They'll not leap the leap
again!"
Said the Lady Eleanora,
Lovely Lady Eleanora von Alleyne!

Came other knights anon to ride around the parapet,
For Lady Eleanora von Alleyne.
Came other knights anon to ride around the parapet,
Till six and thirty corses of both mangled men
and horses
Had been sacrificed as victims at the fane
Of the Lady Eleanora,
Stately Lady Eleanora von Alleyne!

Part Two

The Highway to Gratz

The story reached at Gratz the gallant Margrave
Gondibert
Of Lady Eleanora von Alleyne.
The story reached at Gratz the gallant Margrave
Gondibert
Quoth he, "I trow the woman must be more or
less than human;
She is worth a little peaceable campaign,
Is the Lady Eleanora,
Is the Lady Eleanora von Alleyne!"

He trained a horse to pace round narrow stones laid merlonwise,
For Lady Eleanora von Alleyne.
He trained a horse to pace round narrow stones laid merlonwise,
"Good Gray! do thou thy duty, and this rocky-bosomed beauty
Shall be taught that all the vauntings are in vain
Of the Lady Eleanora,
Of the Lady Eleanora von Alleyne!"

Part Three

The Courtyard of the Lady Eleanor's Castle

He left his castle-halls, he came to Lady Eleanor's.
The Lady Eleanora von Alleyne.
He left his castle-halls, he came to Lady Eleanor's,
"O, lady, best and fairest, here am I,—and, if thou carest,
I will gallop round the parapet amain,
Noble Lady Eleanora,
Noble Lady Eleanora von Alleyne!"

She saw him spring to horse, that gallant Margrave Gondibert,
The Lady Eleanora von Alleyne.
She saw him spring to horse, that gallant Margrave Gondibert.

"O, bitter, bitter sorrow! I shall weep for this
tomorrow!
It were better that in battle he were slain,"
Said the Lady Eleanora,
Said the Lady Eleanora von Alleyne.

Then rode he round and round the battlemented
parapet,
For Lady Eleanora von Alleyne.
Then rode he round and round the battlemented
parapet:
The Lady wept and trembled, and her paly face
resembled,
As she looked away, a lily wet with rain;
Hapless Lady Eleanora!
Hapless Lady Eleanora von Alleyne!

Yet rode he round and round the battlemented
parapet,
For Lady Eleanora von Alleyne.
Yet rode he round and round the battlemented
parapet.
Meanwhile her terror shook her—yea, her breath
well nigh forsook her.
Fire was burning in the bosom and the
brain
Of the Lady Eleanora,
Of the Lady Eleanora von Alleyne!

Then rode he round and off the battlemented
parapet

To Lady Eleanora von Alleyne.
Then rode he round and off the battlemented parapet.
"Now blest be God for ever! This is marvelous! I never
Cherished hope of laying eyes on thee agayne,"
Cried the Lady Eleanora,
Joyous Lady Eleanora von Alleyne!

"The Man of Men thou art, for thou hast fairly conquered me,
The Lady Eleanora von Alleyne!
The Man of Men thou art, for thou hast fairly conquered me.
I greet thee as my lover, and, ere many days be over,
Thou shalt wed me and be Lord of my domain,"
Said the Lady Eleanora,
Said the Lady Eleanora von Alleyne.

Then bowed the graceful knight, the gallant Margrave Gondibert,
To Lady Eleanora von Alleyne.
Then bowed that graceful knight, the gallant Margrave Gondibert,
And thus he answered coldly, "There be many who as boldly
Will adventure an achievement they disdain,

For the Lady Eleanora,
For the Lady Eleanora von Alleyne.

"Mayest bide until they come, O stately Lady Eleanor!
O, Lady Eleanora von Alleyne!
Mayest bide until they come, O stately Lady Eleanor!
And thou and they *may* marry, but, for me, I must not tarry,
I have won a wife already out of Spain."

2. THE PROUD PRINCESS

A PANTOMIME WITH RHYMES*

CHARACTERS:

The Child with the Fairy Book.
The good King Most Polite.
The Proud Princess Rudie—*His daughter*.
The Heralds.
The Pages.

The Suitors:
- The Fat Prince.
- The Thin Prince.
- The Pale Prince.
- The Blushing Prince.
- The King with the Beard—*King Kindly*.

The Priest
Country folk, courtiers, court ladies, musicians, singers—as desired.
The Cook.

COSTUMES:

The costumes are the usual fairy-tale costumes.

For the Princess a flowing robe, a low crown over a thin gauzy scarf and many jewels in the

* Adapted from the prose of *King Grisly Beard* by the Brothers Grimm.

first scene. For the latter scenes her ragged dress may be contrived of large towels or lengths of muslin basted or pinned together.

The two kings have long robes, long cloaks and high crowns. King Kindly has a beard in the first scene but is clean-shaven thereafter. As a beggar he wears a tattered blouse and breeches. The father of the Princess should be made up as a very old man.

The princes who are suitors should wear knee breeches and blouses with gay ribbons around knees, waist or across one shoulder, according to the fancy of the individual prince. They should have short cloaks and may have hats with long plumes.

The heralds may wear long hose over colored trunks (bathing suit trunks have been known to serve well) or knickers, blouses (shirts with attached collars turned back from the throat) short capes from one shoulder, long-plumed hats. (Plumes may be made of crepe or newspaper.)

The pages wear trunks or knickers, long hose and over their blouses straight panels hanging from shoulder to half-way between hip and knee. These panels may be of newspaper as a play upon the word page.

The priest has a black robe with a white surplice.

The men of the country folk may wear knickers and blouses, the women short full skirts, white blouses with laced dark girdles over them and short colored aprons.

The Cook may be man or woman in conventional white cook's garb. There may be kitchen maids in country dress with aprons, or you may see only the cook and assume that the kitchen maids are in another room.

The musicians will wear adaptations of the herald's costumes without the cloak and hats. Courtiers and court ladies wear costumes similar to those of the Princes and the Princess.

The Child with the Fairy Book will be a large young person dressed as a very small boy or girl in modern dress. The Fairy Book should be quite large with a copy of the rhymes fastened on its pages so that they can be read.

SCENERY:

No special scenery is needed as the child will announce the place in which the action of each chapter occurs. Two chairs placed close together and covered with curtains, rugs or blankets will make thrones for the two court scenes. For the kitchen scene only a low stool, a knife and bowl of onions is needed. Of course each scene may be elaborately furnished if desired.

ACTION:

The Child with the Fairy Book is seated at the

front of the stage as far to right or left as is possible. He should be in a position to be seen and heard clearly but should not block off the view of the other players. Usually it is best for him to sit upon a low stool. He reads the first stanza then the curtain rises to show the King upon his throne. If there is no curtain the Child waits until the King enters and is seated before continuing to read.

After that the action is indicated by the rhyme. The Child should read slowly and clearly and should pause for the laughter of the audience. Frequently pantomimes with readings are spoiled because the reader goes right on regardless of the players. Where they are slow in entering or beginning a bit of stage business he should pause and seem to be studying the book—thrilled or excited at what is coming next.

In Chapter One let the page bring in the Princess and let her protest against marriage before Prince Puddinghead is announced. Each of the suitors should be announced by the heralds with a flourish of trumpets (silent, of course) and should kneel before the Princess with violent gestures of devotion. When the Thin Prince falls dead the heralds should carry him out. When the Princess laughs at King Kindly and the priest is summoned she should appear indifferent to King Most Polite's threat. When the beggar appears and the King orders the ceremony to begin she must weep and protest violently.

Chapter Two

Have a group of country people enter from left laughing and happy, the Princess and the beggar enter very wearily from the right. The Princess listens to the happy chatter then slowly goes out at left, weeping. The country people go off at right. To give color to the scene the country people can carry eggs, vegetables or even lead a cow. For costuming cow and making its head see page 11.

Chapter Three

Show the Cook mixing something in a bowl when a page enters with a long scroll—the royal order to the Cook. The Cook expresses despair then the Beggar brings in the Princess. He explains to the Cook that she is a new kitchen maid, the Cook is delighted, the Princess overwhelmed with horror. After insisting that she must stay the Beggar goes out, the Cook brings the onions and the Princess sits down on the stool and weeps as she works. The Princess may have a sponge to be squeezed for tear drops or a handful of paper tears to let fall frequently.

Chapter Four

After reading the fourth line the Child may pause while the musicians play and the singers sing—silently, of course, giving them time to elaborate upon their parts a little before going on with the reading. From this point the action is very clearly indicated by the rhyme. The Child should pause after "Must dance no matter how sad she's feeling" to give the Princess enough time for her dance. Then there is the stately entrance of the King, the dismay of the Princess, his summoning her to his side and a final embrace after she promises to be meek in the future.

The Child [*Reading*].

I'll read to you from my Fairy Book
The terrible fate which overtook
A Princess who was vain and proud
And said ill-mannered thing *out loud!*

Chapter One. The Palace of King Most Polite.

The King was seated upon his throne,
Nodding a bit, for he was alone,
And a golden crown is an awful weight
For one who must always appear in state.
When all at once there came to the King
A herald who said, "My lord, I bring,
Greetings from young Prince Puddinghead
Who comes with hope to your daughter wed."
The King replied, "Bid him enter, pray!"
And ordered the pages without delay
To bring the Princess there to decide
If she wished to be this Prince's bride.

The Princess came in a silken gown
But her face was puckered up in a frown,

"Why must I marry," the Princess pouted.
"I'll have no old-maid daughter!" her father
shouted.
So the Princess sat by her Father's side,
And, "Behold Prince Puddinghead!" heralds
cried.

The Princess took just a single look
Then she laughed 'till the walls of the palace
shook
"He's as round as a tub," laughed she.
"Enough!"
Prince Puddinghead cried and went off in a huff.

Then the King commanded "Usher in
A suitor who is tall and thin!"
So a tall thin prince bowed low and sighed
"Dear Princess, come and be my bride."
"Why you'd make a good Maypole!" the Princess cried.
Which so grieved the Prince that he forthwith
died!

Then the good King shouted in awful rage——
"You unmannerly miss, try to act your age!
This rudeness of yours will quite upset
All the rulings of royal etiquette."
The Princess merely stifled a yawn——
And sighed—"Bring the rest of the suitors on!"

The next Prince in size was exactly right

But he wouldn't do for he looked too white.
Quoth the Princess, "He's pale as a garden wall,
As a husband he just won't do at all!"
And the next Prince, too, she refused to wed,
"He's as red as a cockscomb," the Princess said.
At the next one she laughed 'till she couldn't stop,
"Why, King Kindly's beard's like a kitchen
mop!"

Her father was angry through and through.
"You conceited Princess, I'll settle you.
I'll teach you to turn away in scorn
From Princes and Kings who are nobly born.
For wed you shall be ere this day is o'er,
To the first ragged beggar who comes to our
door!"
And though the Princess wept and wept
The angry King his promise kept.
And when a beggar-man came that way
He was wed to the Princess without delay.

Chapter Two—On the Road in King Kindly's Country

And so, I am sorry to relate
The Princess fell from her high estate
And was doomed to beg for her daily bread
And sleep on a rock for a feather-bed!
And wherever they begged, in village or town,
Was King Kindly held in high renown.
"A King," said the people, "So good and kind
You can travel the world o'er and never find."

"Alas, alas," wept the Princess, "He
Would have been good and kind to me."

Chapter Three—King Kindly's Kitchen

In King Kindly's kitchen excitement reigned
For the King most royally entertained
And word had come to the Cook, "Prepare
New and wonderful dishes of royal fare
With plenty of spices and onions fine
For guests come soon with the King to dine!"
The Cook in distress tore out his hair
And wailed and shrieked his high despair.
"The kitchen maids have enough to do!
Who will peel the onions to season the stew?"
Then into the kitchen the beggar brought
The poor tired Princess, "You must be taught
To cook and bake as a poor wife should,
Here you stay 'till your cooking is really good!"
And off he strode 'though her tears fell fast
And the Cook cried, "An onion peeler at last!"
Behold, then, the once haughty Princess sat,
Peeling an onion and watering it
With tears that fall with every sigh
"Ah, how bitterly punished for pride am I."

Chapter Four—King Kindly's Throne Room

Here is the throne room of Kindly, the King,
Whose praises his people love to sing
For he punishes only the haughty and proud,
Who say ill-mannered things *right out loud.*

The musicians play and the singers sing,
But the throne is empty, where *is* the King?
Each Court-lady powders behind her fan
For the King is a good-looking bachelor man.
Then in comes a Herald, announcing clear,
"On with the dance 'till the King appear.
And for your pleasure and your delight
The Onion Peeler shall dance tonight!"

The courtiers laugh at this merry chance
To see an Onion Peeler dance,
And the poor Princess, wearied from onion peeling
Must dance no matter how sad she's feeling.
Then all at once there's a joyous din,
"The King!" cries the Herald and ushers in——
Clad in the kingly robes and crown
The man who had begged from town to town,
With the poor, proud Princess, who through her tears
Stares in dismay as the King appears.
But he beckons her to his royal throne
And, as meek she approaches, says low, "My own,
My own dear Princess, you're cured of pride,
Come take your place at your husband's side.
To test your manners I first appeared
Disguised by a most unattractive beard
But my new Gillette took the beard off clean
And I then appeared in the humble mien

Of the beggar—and now, you your trials past,
I appear in my rightful guise at last!"

Then, sitting down on the royal throne
The new Queen murmured, "I should have known,
That no ordinary beggar man was he
Who could make an Onion Peeler of me!
And I promise, oh King, for the rest of my life
To be your most loving obedient wife."

V

A HUNGARIAN TRAGEDY

The Kidnapped Bride

V

A HUNGARIAN TRAGEDY

THE KIDNAPPED BRIDE

CHARACTERS:

The Servant.
The Terrible Tartar.
The Lord.
The Lady.

COSTUMES:

The Servant. Trousers tucked into high boots. Tunic with full skirt reaching to calf of legs. Short coat shaped like a bolero. Round brimless hat about six inches high with feather fastened to one side.

The Terrible Tartar. Trousers tucked into boots. Tunic to hips made of gray cambric, oilcloth or paper to imitate a metal corselet or tunic of fur (if there is an old fur rug handy). Round shield, long curving sword and tall cone-shaped hat with about five-inch brim of cloth or fur turned up against the crown. Long beard with fierce mustache.

The Lord. Long tunic reaching to calves, ankle

length, loose sleeved coat bordered with fur. Wide girdle worn outside the coat and wrapped twice around the body, once at waist and once at hips. He has a mustache.

The Lady. Long full dress with square neck and tightly fitted bodice laced in the front with jewels. Waistline tapering to a point at the front. A low crown holding on head a long scarf which trails to the floor.

The colors of all the costumes should be very bright with plenty of red and green.

SETTING:

A room in the Lord's castle. Very little furniture: a high backed chair and a heavy table with a long bench before it will be all that is needed. On the table should be a box painted to imitate an old chest. A very large box imitating another chest should be on the floor. The Lord should have a huge key-ring with keys of various sizes. One huge one should be supposedly the key of the large chest, another key should be for a door (real or only indicated with screens) into an inner room.

[*The curtain rises to discover the Lord polishing his sword.*]

[*Enter the Servant, breathless and bedraggled. He kneels before the Lord.*]

The Lord [*Impatiently*]. Speak! Have you good news or ill?

Servant [*Gasping*]. Ill news, my Lord. Most grievous news.

The Lord [*Shaking him*]. Then let me know the worst at once. Speak!

Servant. My Lord, the Magyars have been defeated. Tartars are not a furlong behind me. The Tartar Khan and his men ride like devils across our plains. They have killed all the men and carried off all the women of our valley, looted and burned every castle. Oh, my Lord, they will be upon us here even while I warn you.

The Lord. God be merciful!

[*He strides back and forth.*]

Life is sweet. I will not defend my castle. Perchance if I offer the great Khan all my treasures he will spare my life. Go bid the guard lower the drawbridge and retire to the guard room. Bid all the servants to welcome the Tartars with bows and smiles. Go, I say!

[*The Servant, trembling, goes out. The Lord quickly locks the door to the inner room then unlocks the chests. From the one on the table he takes necklaces and golden coins and scatters them by the chest on the table. From the one on the floor he pulls out silks and furs and drapes them over the side, temptingly. He fingers his sword then takes it off and places it on the table. He walks up and down nervously. There is loud tapping on the inner door.*]

The Lord [*At the door*]. Be still, my love, I have locked you in to save you from the terrible Tartar!

[*Great noise outside. Shouts. Scuffling. Enter the Tartar.*]

The Lord. Enter, most noble Khan! This castle is yours and I am your loyal servant.

[*The Tartar looks at him, grunts loudly but makes no reply except to finger his sword in a threatening manner.*]

The Lord [*Eagerly*]. Will you not choose from my humble store what pleases you? Here is gold——

[*The Tartar fingers it contemptuously.*]

Here are jewels——

[*The Tartar pushes them aside angrily.*]

Here are furs, my Lord. Bearskins from the great forests beyond the river Don. Silks are here from beyond the seas——

[*The Tartar grunts angrily, draws his sword and is about to kill the Lord when he notices the door. He tries it, finds it locked.*]

The Tartar. What is beyond the door?

The Lord [*Trembling*]. Nothing, my lord.

The Tartar [*Furiously*]. Open at once or——!

[*The Lord opens the door and the Lady comes out.*]

The Tartar. Ah!

The Lord. My lord, she is my wife.

The Tartar. Bah! I take her.

[*He seizes her by the waist and takes her out

with difficulty as she struggles violently. The Lord, thrust back by the Tartar's sword can only watch them go. There is a sound of shouts outside then hoof-beats dying away in the distance. When silence comes the Lord kneels and raises pious eyes toward heaven.]

The Lord.

Heaven has heard my prayer
Heaven has spared my life,
My silks, my gold, my jewels,
True—the Tartar *has* taken my wife.
But——

[*He pauses, then continues.*]

God pity the Tartar!

VI

A LITTLE STUNT FROM ITALY

The Generous Fisherman

VI

A LITTLE STUNT FROM ITALY

THE GENEROUS FISHERMAN

CHARACTERS:

The Nobleman.
The Guests.
The Steward.
The Fisherman.
The Porter.

COSTUMES:

The Nobleman. Long-sleeved doublet and two-colored hose, hair to shoulders or bobbed. Low-pointed shoes. (Bed-room slippers of the Romeo type will do.) Jeweled neck chain.

The Guests. Men dressed like the nobleman in various colors. Woman's costume, long gown fitted to the figure and with train from the shoulder. Hair held in place by a net of jewels.

The Steward. Bright colored smock belted in at waist, V neck edged with fur (may be absorbent cotton tacked on with yarn or thread). Wears long chain and has bunch of keys hanging from belt.

The Porter. Like the steward in style but dull colored smock turned in at neck—no fur.

The Fisherman. Straight, sleeveless, belted tunic of rough cloth. No stockings. The fish may be cut from cardboard and should be enormous in size and a vivid color, pink, red or blue.

As the curtain rises the guests are seated around a long table on which appear bowls of fruit and glasses. It is the end of the feast. The guests may be laughing and talking merrily, or they may be listening to some musicians playing violins or mandolins.

[*Enter the Steward.*]

Steward [*Bowing before the nobleman*]. Senor, there is at the gate a fisherman.

The Guests. But the feast is ended, we need not fish.

The Steward. Senor, it is the largest fish in the world!

A Woman Guest. I want to see the largest fish in the world!

Nobleman. Bid the fisherman bring in his fish.

[*The Steward goes out, returning at once with the fisherman and his fish. He bows before the company.*]

Fisherman. Senor, the most beautiful fish ever caught!

Nobleman. A fine fish indeed. And you will sell it for——

A Guest. He'll ask a fortune for so huge a fish!

Fisherman. I will not accept gold for it, nor jewels.

Nobleman. Are you mad? What will you sell it for?

Fisherman. One hundred blows with a whip.

Guests.

One hundred blows!
The man is mad!
Let us see him get paid!

Nobleman. Steward, take the fish to the cook and bring back a whip.

[*The Steward goes out and returns with the whip.*]

Nobleman. Begin the payment.

[*The Steward cracks the whip loudly but does not hit the fisherman. The guests count in chorus up to fifty.*]

Fisherman. Stop!

[*The Steward stops and the guests look on in astonishment.*]

Fisherman. The other fifty blows belong to the Porter at Senor's gate.

Nobleman. What mean you?

Fisherman. The Porter, Senor, would not let me in to sell my fish until I agreed to give him half of what you paid me.

Guests.

A noble fisherman!
To punish the wicked Porter he bore half the blows.

Here, fisherman, a gold coin for your courage!

Nobleman. Bring in the Porter.

[*The Steward goes out and returns with the Porter.*]

Nobleman. You have been grafting from the tradesmen.

Porter. Senor!

Nobleman. But this generous fisherman insists that you get half of what I paid him.

[*The Porter grins happily.*]

Guests [*Laughing*].

The generous fisherman!
The Porter gets his half!
Pay him!

Porter. Senor, what comes to me? Half of how much money?

Fisherman. Half of one hundred blows from the whip!

Nobleman. Pay him his share!

[*The Porter struggles but the Steward holds him fast. The whip descends and the Porter screams as the curtain falls.*]

VII

A THRILL FROM JAPAN

The Awful Fate of a Fibber

VII

A THRILL FROM JAPAN

THE AWFUL FATE OF A FIBBER!*

CHARACTERS:

The Judge.
Two Devils.
The Recorder.
The Woman.

COSTUMES:

The Judge and the Recorder are in the usual Japanese men's kimonos. That of the Judge is of bright color; the Recorder's, black.

The Woman. Japanese kimono, any color.

The Devils may wear the usual costume of tights and close-fitting tunic with long, close sleeves and head covering with horns and an opening for the face. One should be black, the other red. Or they may wear grinning devil's heads made like an animal's head as described on page —.

SETTING:

A background of screens or plain curtains. At

* From the Japanese Kyogen pantomime—*The River of Fate.*

the center, rear, is the cushion on which the Judge sits. At the right, rear, is a huge kettle with fire under it. The kettle must be large enough to hold the woman and may be cut out of black cardboard and so arranged that only one side shows, or it may be contrived of paper or muslin over a foundation of almost anything, little chairs arranged in a semi-circle, for instance. The flames are red paper.

ACTION:

[*The Judge is discovered seated on his cushion. He must learn to sit on his heels in true Japanese fashion. The devils crouch on each side of the kettle, blowing at the flames.*]

Judge. Is there none coming today across the river which separates life from death?

Black Devil [*Jumping up and running to kneel before the Judge*]. There is one, Excellency. A woman only.

Judge. Bring her before me at once.

[*The Black Devil orders the Red Devil to fetch the woman. The Red Devil goes out and returns dragging the woman by her wrists. She is terribly afraid and falls on her knees before the Judge.*]

Red Devil. Here she is, Excellency!

Judge. Are you a sinner?

Woman [*Trembling*]. Oh, no! most gracious Judge.

Judge. Bring the Keeper of the Book!

[*The Red Devil goes out and returns with the Recorder who kneels before the Judge, opens his book and read.*]

Recorder. This woman told fibs, Excellency. Black fibs and white fibs and gray fibs.

[*The Devils rub their hands and jump about gleefully.*]

Judge. Pull out her tongue!

[*The Devils bring an enormous pair of tweezers. While the Red Devil holds the struggling woman the Black Devil pulls out her tongue. (It is of flannel or paper and amazingly long.)*]

Judge. Complete her punishment.

[*The devils fan the flames beneath the kettle, test the water with their fingers, then suck their fingers to cool them. The water is terribly hot. Then they put the woman in the kettle. She screams and screams then the screams grow faint and cease. The Black Devil peeps into the kettle and beckons to the Red Devil.*]

Judge. Is the punishment complete? Has she been boiled down?

Black Devil. Yes, Excellency.

Judge. Let me see.

[*The Devils stand on tiptoe and reach into the kettle. Then they pull out a very small Japanese doll.*]

Red Devil. Here she is, Excellency.

Judge. She is yours to play with. So perish all who tell fibs—black fibs, white fibs or gray fibs.

[*Each devil takes a hand of the doll and they dance as*]

The Curtain Falls.

VIII

FUN FROM NORWAY

The Youth and the North Wind

VIII

FUN FROM NORWAY

THE YOUTH AND THE NORTH WIND*

CHARACTERS:

The Breezes.
The Old Lame Woman.
Her Son.
The North Wind.
Bill, the Goat.
The Common Goat.
The Landlord.
Other Guests.
The Cudgel.
The Princess.

COSTUMES:†

The Breezes. Flowing gowns with long fluttering angel sleeves made of blue and green cheese cloth, or blue and green crepe paper dresses made with many fluttering narrow pointed panels.

* Poem adapted from the poem by John Godfrey Saxe.

† The author is indebted to Letty G. Shugert's *Costumes for Plays and Pageants* for the description of the Norwegian costumes for men and women.

The Old Lame Woman. Long, full, colored skirt. White apron with colored band. Long sleeved waist with girdle-like bodice. Long narrow colored scarf. One end is held tight across forehead from ear to ear, the length hangs down the back.

The Boy
The Landlord } Knee length trousers with
The Guests bright garters below the knee.
White blouse with coat or vest over it. Coat may extend to waist-line or knees. Caps like skating cap but longer and with tassel at the end.

The Cudgel. Brown or black muslin bag almost the height of the wearer with two holes at the bottom for the feet to go through. The bag is gathered at the neck and the arms are kept inside. The bottom should be stuffed with paper to make it look solid all the way up.

The Princess. Long gown girdled at a high waist-line. Crown and flowing hair.

The North Wind. White gown, long white beard. Sparkling imitation snow can be sprinkled over gown.

The Goats. On all fours with gray blankets over them. Heads made according to directions on page 11 with horns added.

The poem chosen for this stunt lends itself admirably to that stunt form which always delights an audience—the form in which the characters say not only the speeches assigned to them but also the description of what they do and how they speak. It adds considerably to the fun to have the North Wind say not merely "I have it not!" but "I have it not, the North Wind growled."

At the beginning of each scene the Breezes run around the stage, whistling and waving their arms. They fasten up the sign which announces what each scene is and blow down the old sign. They also put in place and later remove any necessary furniture. All the action between scenes must be very quick.

The scenes are as follows:

Scene I. The Cottage.
Furnished with table, two chairs or stools.
Bowl on table.

Scene II. The Road.

Scene III. Cave of the North Wind.
The Breezes, facing each other and clasping hands make an arch with their arms over the head of the North Wind who sits on a low stool or box. The sign "Scene II, etc.," dangles from the hands of the Breezes.

Scene IV. The Inn.
Two benches.

Scene V. The Cottage.
Same as Scene I.

Scene VI. The Cave.
Same as Scene III.

Scene VII. The Inn.
Same as Scene IV.

Scene VIII. The Cottage Glorified.
Table as in Scene I but covered with cloth and with flowers in bowl or vase. Cushions on the chair. Two extra chairs added.

ACTION:

The Breezes blow in and hang up the sign for Scene I, then place the furniture and blow out again. They move with gliding steps and waving arms. The Old Woman hobbles in on a cane from right and sits in chair.

Old Woman.

Once on a time—'twas long ago
There lived a worthy dame.

She knocks on the floor with her cane, the Boy enters at right and stands before her. She gestures to him to take bowl and continues to speak.

Who sent her son to fetch some flour,
For she was old and lame.

The Boy rather reluctantly goes out left with the bowl. The Old Woman hobbles out right. The Breezes blow in, remove furniture and hang up the sign for Scene II. The Boy enters at right, slowly carrying the bowl with a little flour in it in his arms.

The Boy.

But while he loitered on the road,

[*Enter the North Wind.*]

North Wind.

The North Wind chanced to stray
Across the careless youngster's path
And stole the flour away.

[*He seizes bowl and runs out left. The Boy weeps.*]

The Boy.

Alas! What shall we do for bread?
Exclaimed the weeping lad.
The flour is gone! The flour is gone!
And it was all we had!

[*He goes out left. The Breezes blow in and remove sign, make arch for North Wind who enters and sits beneath it. Then the Boy enters right.*]

The Boy.

And so he sought the North Wind's cave,
Beside the distant main.
Good Master Boreas, said the lad,
I want my flour again!
'Twas all we had to live upon
My Mother old and I.
Oh! Give us back our flour again
Or we shall surely die!

North Wind.

I have it not, the North Wind growled;
But for your lack of bread

[*He whistles and the goat enters, left, a rope dragging from his neck. The North Wind gives the rope to the Boy.*]

I give to you this little goat,
'Twill serve you well instead.

For you have but to tell him this:
"Make money, Master Bill!"
And he will give you golden coins,
As many as you will.

[*The goat drops a coin from his mouth to the Boy's hand. The boy hugs the goat.*]

The Boy.

The lad received the little goat
With wonder and delight
And thanked the donor heartily,
As well, indeed, he might.

After shaking the North Wind's hand he goes out, right. The Breezes screen the North Wind as he goes out left. They take out his seat and change the signs. The Landlord enters right, serves drinks to the guests who enter right and sit on benches.

The Boy [*Entering at left*].

Returning homeward, at an inn
Just half his journey through
The Boy would show his little goat
And what the goat could do.

[*The Landlord brings him a glass. He takes it then says—Make money, Master Bill!*]

[*The goat drops a coin in the Landlord's hand. All express wonder. The guests and the Landlord go out. The Boy ties the goat to one bench and sleeps on the other. The Landlord enters leading another goat.*]

Landlord.

So while he slept the knavish host

Crept slyly from his bed
And stole the goat, but shrewdly placed
Another in its stead.

[*He exchanges the goats and goes out with the magic goat.*]

[*The Boy gets up, yawns and goes out right with the goat, saying as he goes—*]

The Boy.

Unknowing what the rogue had done
The youth went on his way,
And reached his weary journey's end
Just at the close of day.

[*The Breezes enter and prepare Scene V.*]

[*The Old Woman hobbles in right and sits down.*]

[*The Boy and the goat enter left.*]

The Boy.

He showed the dame his magic goat
And told her of his power.
Good sooth! he cried, 'Twas well for us
The North Wind stole the flour!

Old Woman.

I much misdoubt, the Dame replied,
Your wondrous tale is true,
'Tis little good for hungry folk
Your silly goat can do.

The Boy.

Good Master Bill! the lad exclaimed,
Make money!

The Goat.

But alas,

'Twas nothing but a common goat
And nothing came to pass.

The Old Woman shakes her stick at the Boy and he goes off left with the goat. She hobbles out right. The Breezes set Scene VI with the North Wind as before.

The Boy [*Entering right*].

Then to the North Wind angrily
He sped with might and main
Your foolish goat is good for naught,
I want my flour again!

North Wind.

I have it not, the North Wind growled,
Nor can I give you aught

[*He claps his hand and the Cudgel hops in.*]

Except this Cudgel, which indeed,
A magic charm has got.
For you have but to tell it this,
Good Cudgel, hit away!

[*The Cudgel hits the Boy with its shoulders. The Boy backs away.*]

And 'till you bid it "Stop" again

[*The Cudgel stops and stands very still.*]

The Cudgel will obey.

The Boy shakes the North Wind's hand, takes hold of the Cudgel and goes out right. The Breezes shift the Scene to Scene VII. The Boy enters, greets the Landlord, stands the Cudgel against a bench and lies down on the bench. The Landlord pretends to sleep on the other bench.

The Boy.

Returning home, he stopped at night
Where he had stopped before
And, feigning to be fast asleep
He soon began to snore.

[*The Landlord rises and tiptoes to the Cudgel.*]

The Landlord.

And when the host would steal the staff

The Boy.

The sleeper murmured, Stay,
I see what you would fain to be at!
Good Cudgel, hit away!

Cudgel.

The Cudgel thumped about his ears

Landlord.

Until the rascal said,
I'll give you back your Billy-goat:
Oh, spare my broken head.

The Boy. Stop!

[*The Cudgel stops, the Landlord rushes out right and returns with the goat.*]

The Boy [*Going out right with the goat*].

And so it was the lad reclaimed
His magic Billy Goat.

The Breezes set Scene VIII.

The Old Woman hobbles in right, leading the goat. She sits in a chair, the goat stands behind her with its head on her shoulder. The Boy enters, right. He has a large envelope labeled "Famous" pinned to the front of his cap, or at the front of a felt hat.

The Boy.

The Boy grew rich and soon became
A man of famous note

[*He touches the envelope.*]

He kept his mother tenderly

[*He kisses her.*]

And cheered her waning life.

[*He dances with the goat and she laughs heartily.*]

He married, as you may suppose
A Princess for a wife!

The Princess enters. He takes her hand, leads her to the table, seats her, leans over and kisses her. He seats his Mother, takes his place opposite the Princess. The Goat sits opposite the Old Lady. All fold their hands as if saying grace before meat. The Breezes blow in.

Breezes [*In a wheezy tune*]. The end! The end! The end!

IX

PERSIA PRESENTS

The Bored King and the Bandit

IX

PERSIA PRESENTS

THE BORED KING AND THE BANDIT

(An old Persian Legend dramatized in that very modern stunt form which requires the characters to say much more than an audience usually expects of them.)

CHARACTERS:

The Bored King.
The Princess.
The Chamberlain.
The Steward.
The Chief Slave.
The Bandit.

COSTUMES:

The King. Full trousers gathered at the ankles. A knee length long-sleeved coat over a white blouse and jeweled girdle. A turban fastened with jewels, with feather at the center-front. Slippers without heels. The colors of the king's costume should be very gaudy.

The Steward
The Chamberlain } Same type of costume but less colorful and very small turbans.

The Chief Slave. Short sleeveless tunic, girdle, close fitting turban.

The Bandit. Same type of costume but with short coat, boots and a fez instead of a turban.

STAGE SETTING:

No special scenery is needed for this stunt. The Chief Slave may show the audience a placard at the beginning of each of the three acts which will indicate where the act takes place.

ACT I. The Palace of the King of Persia—Afternoon.

ACT II. The Palace of the King of Persia—The next morning.

ACT III. The Dungeon—15 minutes later.

For Acts I and II there should be a heap of bright colored cushions upon which the King and Princess will be seated.

For Act III the fact that the scene is a dungeon may be indicated by a small grating to represent a window and by the chains with which the Bandit is fastened.

ACTION:

After the Slave has shown the placard announcing the first act the curtain rises discovering the King and the Princess seated upon cushions being fanned by the Chief Slave who wheels a huge long-handled fan.

King. The King is bored says the bored King.

Princess. The Princess is bored also echoes the beautiful Princess daintily stifling a yawn.

King. What can we do for amusement asks the bored King?

Princess. We might announce a new contest for my hand wearily suggests the beautiful Princess.

King. True, agrees the King, but it must be a very difficult contest with death for the losers. Slave! Summon the Chief Steward!

Slave [*Bowing to the King*]. The obedient Slave immediately fetches the Chief Steward.

[*He goes out returning immediately with the Steward.*]

Steward [*The Steward approaches the King in fear and trembling*]. What is your Majesty's desire asks the Steward nervously?

King. What will be served at the royal dinner tonight inquires the King

Steward. Fish your Majesty replies the Steward.

King. Very good says the bored king becoming slightly less bored. See that there is enough fish for one hundred guests and send the Lord Chamberlain to me.

Steward. The Steward hurries off to do the King's bidding says the Steward.

Princess. The beautiful Princess is shaken with curiosity [*She shakes violently*]. What have fish to do with a contest for my hand inquires the beautiful Princess.

King. You shall see replies the bored King becoming less bored every minute.

[*Enter the Chamberlain.*]

Chamberlain. The dutiful Chamberlain approaches the bored King and, bowing low, awaits the King's command.

King. Invite one hundred young men who wish to marry the beautiful Princess to dine at the palace tonight commands the bored King. When the Steward has served the fish watch every guest. Should any guest be so polite that he eats but one side of his fish he may win the hand of the Princess. Those who piggishly eat to the fish bone then turn the fish to eat the other side shall be——

Princess. What, cries the beautiful Princess now very much excited.

King. Beheaded! thunders the bored King.

[*Curtain falls.*]

Act II.

THE PALACE OF THE KING OF PERSIA

The curtain rises discovering the King and the Princess seated as in Act I.

King. The bored King is more bored than ever sighs the bored King.

Princess. Watching ninety-nine men gobble both sides of their fish *is* a bore agrees the beautiful Princess.

King. Seeing ninety-nine men beheaded is a fearful bore yawns the bored King.

[*There is a noise outside.*]

King. Slave see who is making all that commotion commands the bored King.

Slave [*As he goes out*]. The obedient Slave obeys.

[*Slave reenters immediately followed by the Chamberlain, and the Steward holding the struggling Bandit.*]

Bandit. The notorious Bandit struggles in the hands of his captors but becomes harmless and meek when his eyes fall upon the beautiful Princess.

[*He drops a pair of large paper eyes in the Princess's lap.*]

Princess. The beautiful Princess forthwith gives her heart to the bold but handsome Bandit.

[*She hands him a huge paper heart.*]

King. What villain have we here thunders the bored King.

Bandit. A most notorious Bandit replies the scoundrel.

King. Off with his head orders the bored King.

Princess. O King beseeches the beautiful Princess at least grant that he may take the fish test first.

King. Agreed says the bored King. Steward bring in the fish.

Steward. At once your Majesty replies the faithful Steward.

[*Steward goes out and returns with a plate containing a slice of bread cut in the shape of a fish.*]

[*The Chamberlain places a low stool in front of the Bandit. He sits on the floor guarded by the Chief Slave with upraised sword.*]

King [*Rising and yawning*]. I am too bored to watch the villain eat says the bored King. Should he fail to meet the test of politeness take him at once to the Dungeon and I will come to see him beheaded. The King stalks out.

Princess. I am too nervous to watch this test says the beautiful Princess following the bored King from the room.

Bandit. The Bandit begins to eat the fish with relish. [*Steward hands him a bottle or jar.*] This is excellent fish says the bold Bandit. He reaches the fish bone and begins to eat the other side of the fish.

Chamberlain
Steward
Slave } He has failed cry the King's faithful servants and hustle the Bandit to the Dungeon to be beheaded.

Act III

THE DUNGEON

The Bandit heavily chained sits upon the floor of Dungeon guarded by the Slave.

[*Enter the Princess.*]

Princess. Hearing the terrible news the beautiful Princess rushes to the side of the bold but handsome Bandit. Oh my love cries the beautiful Princess must you die?

Bandit. Alas replies the notorious Bandit, I must.

[*Enter the King.*]

King. What does this mean shouts the bored King entering in time to see the beautiful Princess kiss the notorious Bandit.

Princess. It means I love the notorious Bandit cries the beautiful Princess defiantly.

King. That's just too bad says the bored King but I have given orders to behead him and a King cannot change his mind.

Princess. The beautiful Princess moans pitifully.

Bandit. The notorious Bandit shakes with anguish.

King. Even the bored King weeps at the sad plight of the lovers. Tell you what I'll do offers the bored King generously. I will grant three wishes before you die.

Bandit. The notorious Bandit cheers up immediately.

King. What is your first wish asks the bored King curiously.

Bandit. Half of your treasure replies the notorious Bandit.

King. It is yours agrees the bored King reluctantly giving the notorious Bandit twenty-six cents. What is your second wish?

Bandit. To marry the beautiful Princess, of course, replies the notorious Bandit.

Princess. Oh goody exclaims the beautiful Princess clapping her hands with joy.

King. You shall marry her as soon as we can get a priest and order her widow's weeds agrees the bored King. What is your third wish?

Bandit. The notorious Bandit thinks deeply. My third wish says the notorious Bandit after much thought is that you put out the eyes of all who saw me eat the fish.

King. It shall be done at once agrees the bored King. Slave who saw the notorious Bandit eat the fish?

Slave. I didn't see it your Majesty cried the Slave it must have been the Steward.

King. Fetch the Steward at once commands the bored King.

Slave. The trembling Slave immediately brings in the faithful Steward.

King. I am going to put out your eyes thunders the bored King. I have promised to put out the eyes of all who saw the notorious Bandit eat the fish.

Steward. I did not see it your Majesty it must have been the Chamberlain protests the faithful Steward.

King. Fetch the Chamberlain commands the bored King.

Steward. The terrified Steward immediately fetches the Chamberlain.

King. I am going to put out your eyes thunders the bored King. I have promised to put out the eyes of all who saw the notorious Bandit eat the fish.

Chamberlain. The Chamberlain grovels at the feet of the King. Oh your Majesty he replies I did not see the notorious Bandit eat the fish. I was taking a cinder out of my eye.

King. The bored King is very much puzzled. This is a very strange situation says the bored King.

Bandit. The notorious Bandit speaks up promptly. As long as nobody saw me commit the crime your Majesty it is proof that I am innocent and must be set free.

King. The bored King scratches his head in perplexity. I guess you're right says the bored King. Strike off his chains.

[*The Slave, the Steward and the Chamberlain eagerly unfasten the chain.*]

Princess [*Embracing the notorious Bandit*]. Now we can live happily ever after cries the beautiful Princess.

Bandit. The notorious Bandit presses the beautiful Princess to his manly bosom. Did anyone ever tell you that you are beautiful he asks passionately.

King. This love stuff bores me more than anything yawns the bored King.

[*Curtain.*]

PART TWO

Parties!

I

WHAT MAKES A PERFECT PARTY?

I

WHAT MAKES A PERFECT PARTY?

What can you do to insure, at the end of the evening, an enthusiastic and sincere

"We've had a perfectly wonderful time!"?

There's a long row of books on the subject stretching before me. If I look at them I shall grow discouraged at the thought of trying to answer the question in less than a whole volume on recreational leadership. But there's a long row of successful parties stretching behind me and as I look at them I know that I can tell you quite briefly what makes a perfect party.

Once in a while a good party just happens. A group gathers spontaneously, everyone is in a jolly mood, almost everyone thinks of something interesting to do, everyone is willing to do it and behold! "A perfectly wonderful time."

But it isn't safe to depend upon miracles and such a party is sheer miracle.

Personally I prefer to have a plan.

If possible, (and it's more often possible than you dare hope until you begin trying it!) I want a perfectly new plan, grown out of an idea that is original or so skillfully adapted that nobody recognizes it. I choose a central idea suggested by the season or the weather or the shape of a poem or the arrangement of the social room to be used and that idea is carried out *with* absolute consistency in every detail of my party-plan. Invitations, decorations, games, stunts, special musical features, refreshments, everything must emphasize that central idea. Nothing will spoil a party more quickly than a jarring note—like serving hot dogs at a Persian Party. It pays to be fussy over trifles if you want to approach perfection as a hostess.

Of course you must choose your idea with your own group in mind. Remember the age and the interests of your guests. Don't plan to include classical music if your guests think *That's My Weakness Now* is "simply swell."

You must make your plan very complete. Know exactly what is going to be done first and next and next. Talk your plan over thoroughly with your social committee if you have one. Assign some specific responsibility to each member of the committee but keep final authority in your own hands. It is fatal to have half a dozen person trying to explain the same part of the program. Make a list of all the properties to be used in games and stunts and appoint one person to secure them. Check with that person before the party begins so that you won't announce Persian Polo and then discover that there are no blown eggs present.

Copy an outline of the program on a small card

which you can keep with you. In your plan provide for (1) a jolly way to get acquainted, (2) a method of dividing into groups if you have a large crowd, (3) careful balance between activities in which all participate and those in which a few amuse or entertain the whole crowd, (4) several more activities than you expect to need so that you can make a last-minute change if the game which was enjoyed in Chicago is a dud in Los Angeles, (5) an unusual manner of securing partners for the refreshment period or manner of serving the refreshments, (6) an effective ending.

Use imagination in large quantities, especially in your decorations and don't lazily suppose that decorations don't matter. They do.

Come to the party expecting to enjoy it, not dreading it as a terrible task. Be enthusiastic but avoid gushing. Don't try to be funny. Don't be bossy. Don't shout directions. State a signal for absolute silence at the beginning of the party —one blast on your whistle or one chord on the piano—and wait until silence comes before beginning to give directions. Be sure you know the directions for the games before the party begins. Keep your temper if there is a "smarty" in the crowd and ignore him. If you notice him, even to scold, you will be playing into his hands.

Stop each game while the guests are enjoying it, don't wait until they begin to tire of it. Let the party end before anyone begins to talk about going home. Have a good party which will make your guests eager to come back, don't try to keep them until they are wishing they had gone to the first show of the "Talkies" and got to bed at a decent hour.

Keep your eyes and ears and note book open for new ideas and try to include something distinctive in each party even if it is only a different way of shaking hands.

The parties which follow are all original and are especially interesting because they are based upon the customs of many countries. You not only play a new game, you get new glimpses of other nations and other races. While planned for large groups of young people they all can be adapted to small groups in a private home.

All of the parties have been proved more than once so I have a reasonable hope that if you use the plans exactly you too will have

"A perfectly wonderful time."

II

A CUPID'S TOUR OF THE WORLD

II

A CUPID'S TOUR OF THE WORLD

This program, which can be amplified, as much as you desire, is based upon quaint customs, superstitions and poetry in various lands, all developed into the kind of activities which have proved popular with American young people. Although especially designed for a St. Valentine's Day Party it can be used with good effect at any season.

Invitations—Using for a pattern the stiff paper Cupids which flood the five-and-ten-cent stores at the Valentine season and an ordinary tumbler, draw on stiff white paper a Cupid holding the globe in his hands. Color the Cupid and lightly indicate countries and parallels on the globe. The same design can be used on posters. On the globe write:

> That Love can make the world go round,
>   Is known by everyone.
> Come tour with Cupid 'round the world
>   And see how it is done.

On the reverse side of the globe write:

Romance Tours, Inc.
D. Cupid, Manager.
Tour leaving ——————
February 14 ——————

Decorations—The entrance to the social hall may represent the office of a steamship company, with imitations of the usual advertising posters on the wall, setting forth the wonders of especially romantic spots, such as Blarney Castle, Ireland, the Road to Mandalay, etc.

Here the guests register for the tour on the steamer "Courtship."

One side of the social hall may represent the deck of the ship, with a rail separating it from the rest of the room and a gang-plank at one end. Deck chairs face the rest of the room. Passengers sit on the deck between games and during special numbers. Lines representing some of the ship's rigging should have red hearts strung upon them and a flag with a heart upon it should be flying.

Members of the social committee may wear white skirts or trousers and middies with red ties and a red heart on the sleeve. Captain D. Cupid himself, the master of ceremonies, conforms to convention sufficiently to wear white trousers and blue coat—also with heart on sleeve—and blue officer's cap. He wears spectacles for his blindness and wee paper wings flutter from his serge-covered shoulders. He must, of course, be a jolly soul and able by his own comments on the lands visited to insure much of the success of the tour.

Program—To the itinerary of the Romance Tours you may add any stop you wish. The following are given merely as suggestions. The order of the journey may seem strange, but remember that the "Courtship" sails on a chart all its own!

With slight modifications the "Cupid's Tour of the World" makes an unusually attractive banquet program. Decorate the tables with small globes on stands with a red cardboard cupid flying over each globe. If the hand of the cupid is caught beneath the rod at the top of the globe you have the effect of cupid poised above the world and turning it with his hand.

Have the songs chosen to represent the different countries on song sheets at each place. Add "Drink to Me Only With Thine Eyes" for England, "The Spanish Cavalier" for Spain. "Mariannina" can be sung for Italy by a male quartet.

The company can visit France while still at tables and the stunts can follow the dinner.

Romance Tour

First Stop—Ireland

Irish Love Songs—"Kathleen Mavourneen," "Come Back to Erin" and "Believe Me, if All Those Endearing Young Charms." Given as instrumental selections.

Scotland

Love Songs—"Annie Laurie" and "The Blue Bells of Scotland." Solos in costume.

England

Game—Lover's Sighs. Based upon Shakespeare's line: "And then the lover, sighing like a furnace."

The girls work in pairs, one girl of each pair being blindfolded, the other furnished with pencil and paper. All the boys stand in a row and each couple of girls must walk along the row, the blindfolded girl trying to guess the identity of the boys by their deep sighs. The boys are numbered and the guesses recorded by the blindfolded girl's partner. The couple with most correct guesses to its credit is awarded a box of candy hearts.

One of Shakespeare's love scenes can be enacted while in England or some of his love songs* sung or a guessing game played which tests the travelers' knowledge of the famous lovers in his plays.

The stunt play, Pyramis and Thisbe which Shakespeare includes in "A Midsummer Night's Dream" Act V, Scene I could be used.

France

The Court of Love—Following the charming old French custom, a number of girls are selected to form the "Court of Love" and seated in places of honor. They act as judges upon questions of gallantry brought to them. A proper modern question might be, "Should a modern girl pay her

* See *A Book of Shakespeare's Songs*—Edwards. Published by Theodore Presser, Philadelphia.

share of the expenses of a 'date' if she earns as much money as the man who escorts her?" "Should women propose and how?" These questions are debated by several of the boys, the "Court" acting as judge. Then comes the hearing of the minstrels—a number of the boys in turn sing a verse of a well-known love song and the "Court" awards a laurel wreath (paper) to the best voice or most passionate expression.

Switzerland

Planting of the Pine Tree—Played by any number of couples. Give each girl a Swiss window cut out of cardboard.

To make a window take a sheet of cardboard and cut down the center to within a few inches of top and bottom. At both ends of this cut make a cross cut to within a few inches of each side. Bend back from the center and you will have the effect of a window frame with casements opened outward. A few lines drawn with a crayon will indicate the small panes in each casement.

The girls, stationed in different parts of the room, hold the windows in front of them and sing (Air—Overture from "William Tell")

> I'm standing at my window dear,
> I'm standing in the moonlight clear,
> So plant your tree and have no fear
> I'm waiting for you.

While the girls sing each boy is blindfolded and given a little paper pine-tree with a thumb-tack in the trunk. Then, guided by his own girl's voice, each boy tries to find her window and fasten the tree to the lower part of the frame. But when you are blinded and all the girls are singing at once this is no easy task!

This game is suggested by the Swiss custom of honoring one's love by planting a pine tree beneath her window.

Germany

The Marriage Coop—

"The marriage-state is like a coop built stout,
The outs would fain be in the ins be out."

Old Proverb.

Make of this proverb a variation of the familiar musical games. Call half the tourists "ins" and half "outs." Mark on the floor with chalk or string fairly large triangles representing the coops. While "O Where Has My Little Dog Gone?" is played, let the tourists, hands on hips, skip about the room in any direction, so long as they keep moving. As they skip they sing

"O the marriage state is a sorry state,
It's like a coop builded stout,
All the outs would like to be in, be in,
The ins would like to be out."

When the whistle blows suddenly all the "ins" who are standing on coops must drop out of the game, as must all the "outs" who are not on the coops. The winner, of course, is the player who survives the weeding-out process.

While in Germany the travelers may enjoy either of the romantic stunts in Part One, Chapter V.

Japan

The Squeeze—Groups form four straight lines. At a signal each "end man" squeezes the hand of the player on his right, and so on down the line. When the other "end man" receives the squeeze, he raises his right hand. The winning group is the one whose leader raises his hand first.

Arabia

The stunt, "The Secret of Success" in Part One, Chapter IV makes a fine contribution for Arabia.

Turkestan

The Bride's Hand—"The bridegroom must identify the hand of his bride, whom he has never seen and who stands among a number of women."

Give each girl a sheet of paper on which to trace the outline of her hand. Shuffle the sheets and give one to each boy. When he has found the girl whose hand he holds he has found his partner for the refreshment period.

Refreshments—Fruit punch poured by the nautical social committee out of huge bottles labeled "Love Potion," heart-shaped cookies, candy hearts.

The Home Port

Group singing of a few modern love songs.

Then a not-too-lingering "Good-night."

III

A GOLDEN HOURS PARTY

III

A GOLDEN HOURS PARTY

"TIME, THE OLD GYPSY MAN," IS HOST AT A DELIGHTFULLY DIFFERENT PARTY

The Golden Hours Party grew out of a thought suggested by Ralph Hodgson's poem

"Time, you old gypsy-man
Will you not stay?
Put up your caravan
Just for a day?"

It can be given at any season of the year, indoors or out-of-doors. It is especially pleasant indoors in January when the world outside is rather dreary.

Invitations. On yellow-tinted paper.

"Time, the Old Gypsy Man
Promised to stay
To put up his caravan
While young folks play
Come on the chosen night
(Through snow or showers)
Come and share our delight
In Time's golden hours."

Place ————————
Date ————————
Gypsy Costume R.S.V.P.

The color scheme of the social hall will be a soft, glowing yellow with touches of tinsel gilt. The lights should be shaded with yellow and yellow paper blossoms and inexpensive toy canaries may add to the gay tone. An imitation sun-dial near the door (a high, round table covered with crepe paper with a gilt pasteboard indicator and markings in black) will bear the legend, "I mark but sunny hours." At the front of the room should hang Time's Magic Clock, cut from cardboard and decorated with gilt. There should be movable hands so that Time may indicate the beginning of each new division of the program.

"Time, the Old Gypsy Man" is master of ceremonies and will wear gypsy head-dress of yellow, yellow waist-scarf and black ear-rings. A black beard will be effective. His assistants should have costumes suggestive of gypsies but should confine themselves to yellow with touches of black and possibly sky blue. The gypsy costume for the social committee will add tremendously to the festive spirit and can be created easily with the aid of crepe paper or yellow dyed cheesecloth. A gypsy tent—evidently erected for only a short stay—may be a part of the decorations and a place to keep materials for the games or a place from which to serve refreshments.

Gypsy costume for the guests will be optional with the hosts. You may prefer to let your guests come in ordinary clothes. Gypsy costumes are easy to contrive, however, and will add to the gayety of the guests as well as to the picturesque effect of the scene.

Refreshments may be little yellow cakes and candies and orange punch served from a golden gypsy cauldron. (A kettle covered with yellow paper, hanging on a three-legged tripod.)

The guests will be greeted by Time's gypsy assistants. If the party is very large there may be twelve Hours to assist him, each one to be responsible for a part of the program. Ordinarily three or four assistants will be plenty. When the guests have all arrived Time will come out of his tent and announce——

"I Time, the Old Gypsy Man
Promised to stay
Here with the young folks
For one golden day
Let's make each moment count
Come! Let us play!"

Then he moves the hands of the clock to the first golden hour. The hours suggested may be modified greatly to suit the wishes of any local group. Make each hour brief. Here are the twelve——

The Exercise Hour.
The Fashion Hour.
The Children's Hour.
The Lost Hour.
The Oriental Hour.
The Hour of Drama.
The Music Hour.

The Hour of Judgment.
The Hour of Punishment.
The Refreshment Hour.
The Story Hour.
The Fortune Hour.

The Exercise Hour.

To make ready for the strenuous day, of course. The guests will be lined up for "Upsetting exercises" and given the official position—"Toes together, fingers at ears," which they must assume upon command "Position." The exercises may include eye-winking, ear-wiggling. The frog-dance step, hands on hips, rise on toes, deep-knee bend, jump up on heels with out-flung arms, can be attempted to the music of "Jump, Sang the Little Mister Bull-frog." If preferred, some rhythmic dances or group folk dances may be used in this hour.

The Fashion Hour.

The guests are paired off by a march at the end of the exercise hour and each guest is given a yard-long strip of yellow crepe paper—the widest of the streamer type rolls—about four inches wide will do. With this paper and two pins each girl guest will make a necktie for her partner who will in turn design a head-dress for her. Infinite variety in head-dress is possible, gypsy roses behind one ear, French maid's caps, pert Alsatian bows, etc., will appear in the fashion parade. The most stylish couple will, of course, be given a slight reward. Perhaps golden watches from the Five and Ten Cent Store.

The Children's Hour.

Time and his assistants will conduct a brief contest in spinning tops, skipping rope, playing "jacks" and shooting marbles. A harmonica contest may be substituted for the games.

The Lost Hour.

"Lost" announces Time sadly, "Somewhere between sunrise and sunset, sixty golden minutes set with sixty diamond seconds. No reward is offered but we'll see if they can be found."

Sixteen guests line up in groups of four and attempt to restore the lost hour. They line up, Indian file behind a line called sunrise and must race to a goal called sunset over four narrow tracks marked by chalk or strings. They race in relay fashion, each racer moving backward toward the goal and stopping to pick up fifteen grains of corn (real or candy) which he must carry to sunset and then, still moving backward, give to the next member of his team. No receptacle is provided for the grains—the racers must carry them in their hands. The first team to have its fourth member deposit sixty grains at sunset will, of course, have restored the lost hour.

The Oriental Hour.

Big Lantern, Little Lantern. Japanese words; Okii Chochin (Okey Chockin), Chiisai Chochin (Cheese Sigh Chockin). Players gather in circle, a leader in the center. When the leader, forming a small lantern with his hands, says "Okii Chochin!" (Large Lantern), the players must form a large lantern with their hands. When the leader forming a large lantern with his hands, says, "Chiisai Chochin!" (Little lantern), the players must form a small lantern. Leader may thus give one command and execute another. Players must obey the command only. The player who makes the first mistake is "it." (Japanese)

Japanese Spoon Race. Groups line up shoulder to shoulder, each group having one of its members stationed several yards in front of the line. At the signal, the first player in each line takes a teaspoon on which he carries a ball and runs around the team member who is stationed in the front, returning to hand the spoon and ball to the next player in line. Each player must pass around the man who is placed in front of the line and must return to the starting place if he drops the ball. The group in which all the players finish first is, of course, the winner.

Chinese Chicken. Each player removes one shoe, and the shoes are arranged in a straight line at intervals of about two feet. The chicken then hops on one foot to the end of the line where, with his lame foot he kicks away the last shoe in line, then picks it up and carries it back along the same route to the other end of the line where he may kick away and pick up a second shoe before returning. He may touch only one foot to the ground and may touch it but once in each interval. He must not touch any shoe except the ones at each end of the line, and he must pick up the shoes he has kicked away without putting his lame foot on the ground. Nor will the chicken be allowed to drop any of the shoes which he is carrying. When the chicken violates any of these rules, he must at once give place to another performer. The winner is the one who has the greatest number of shoes at the end of the game. Owners may regain their shoes by paying any forfeit suggested by the winner.

These games are merely suggestive. This hour might be representative of any other country.

The Hour of Drama.

Here present in pantomime, accompanied by a reading or solo, the "Wraggle-Taggle Gypsies—O." Exaggerate all the emotions shown, especially the grief of the lord and the disdain of the lady. The song, with music is given here——

4 The Lord:
Come, saddle to me my milk-white steed,
And go and fetch my pony, O!
That I may ride and seek my bride,
Who is gone with the wraggle-taggle gypsies, O!

5 Then he rode high, and he rode low,
He rode through wood and copses too,
Until he came to an open field,
And there he espied his a-lady, O!

6 The Lord:
What makes you leave your house and land?
What makes you leave your money, O!
What makes you leave your new wedded lord,
To go with the wraggle-taggle gypsies, O?

7 The Lady:
O what care I for my house and land?
What care I for my money, O?
What care I for my new wedded lord?
I'm off with the wraggle-taggle gypsies, O!

8 The Lord:
Last night you slept on a goose-feather bed,
With the sheet turned down so bravely, O!
But to-night you'll sleep in a cold open field,
Along with the wraggle-taggle gypsies O!

9 The Lady:
O what care I for a goose-feather bed,
With the sheet turned down so bravely, O!
For to-night I shall sleep in a cold open field,
Along with the wraggle-taggle gypsies, O!

The Music Hour.

The Music Hour may be a separate hour or combined with the Hour of Drama, that is, there may be pantomimes illustrative of the songs.

Musical numbers may include the delightful gypsy song, "The Gypsy Trail" by Kipling and Galloway which makes a fine solo or male chorus. So does "Where My Caravan Has Rested" by Herman Lohr. Victor Herbert's popular "Slumber On, My Little Gypsy Sweetheart" can be used with good effect.

The song "Play Gypsies, Dance Gypsies" from The Countess Maritza makes a very effective number for gypsy singers and dancers with violin accompaniment.

The Hour of Judgment.

All during the evening the guests have looked curiously at the gold stars worn by a few of their number but no questions regarding the stars have been answered. Now Time calls the star-wearing folk to the front. Each one reads a list of guests who are summoned by Time. When the guests so summoned are before Time he tells them that the gold star folk, the Gloom Detectors, have caught these guests in at least one grumble. It may have been a very little grumble, such as "I wish we'd play another game" or "this room is too warm" but each grumbler will be sentenced to do a stunt to redeem himself and to wear a long black crepe for the rest of the evening. It is surprising how frequently even the Gloom Detectors are caught by each other.

The Hour of Punishment.

The Hour of Punishment is, of course, the period in which the culprits carry out the sentences imposed upon them. The sentences may be in the nature of individual performances, such as (1) Pay a compliment to every blue-eyed girl in the room. (2) Measure the combined footage of all the brown-haired men (Take the length of one foot for each man on a long string. Usually a small ball of string is best). (3) Draw a picture of Time on a blackboard or poster. (4) Imitate, in pantomime, two gypsies trying to trade horses.

If preferred, the punishments of the gypsy men may be in the nature of contests between the culprits, such as comical wrestling matches, rooster fights and other contests of strength, or races, such as an Eskimo race on all fours with stiff joints* or a Japanese crab race backward on all fours with elbows and knees bent.

The Refreshment Hour.

Time for serving the refreshments already suggested, a time which may be accompanied by——

The Story Hour.

In which one or two short stories of Gypsy life may be told by Time or one of his assistants. See the Gypsy stories by Konrad Berovici and the volumes of the Gypsy Lore Magazine in the public libraries.

* Described by Jessie H. Bancroft in *Games for the Playground, Home, School and Gymnasium.*

The Fortune Hour.

The Fortune Hour is conducted by one or more very old gypsies who, when their palms are crossed with silver will read the palms of the guests or tell their fortunes from tea leaves or cards. Special gypsy fortune-telling cards can be purchased from some of the novelty shops in the larger cities or a set can be made from the pictures in the bound volumes of *The Gypsy Lore Magazine.*

IV

A NIGHT IN WONDER-WANDER LAND

A Japanese Party

IV

A NIGHT IN WONDER-WANDER LAND *

This party had two sources of inspiration. In an old dusty book of Japanese poems I found the first stanza of our invitation. Its almost Japanese lantern shape intrigued me and its subject was made to order for a party invitation. All I had to do was write a second stanza to match it and there was a most alluring invitation. The program grew naturally out of "Old Japan"—that weird land which Alfred Noyes describes in "The Flower of Old Japan."

Invitations. On the inside of tiny colored lanterns, cut double from tinted paper, write the following invitation, changing the date in the second stanza to suit your own plan.

It is an awesome thing
To meet a-wandering
  In the dark night,
The dark rainy night,
A Phantom greenish gray,

* Reprinted from Joy from Japan by permission of the Heidelberg Press.

Ghost of some wight,
Poor mortal wight,
Wandering
Lonesomely
Through
The black
Night!

Yet if in ghostly garb
You will come wandering
In the dark night—
(Say—at eight Friday night)
Down to the church door* glide
Cautiously there abide
Until a ghostly guide
Silently
Lead you where
Japan's
Ghosts
Hide!

Decorations. Here is your supreme chance to let your imagination hold full sway in making your social room or rooms a place of dread and mystery, wonderful to behold. You will, of course, remove all of the usual furniture. Some strips of matting or Crex rugs will take the place of chairs, if indeed the Ghostly Guide gives you much opportunity to sit down. If more than one room can be used, the different places mentioned

* Or wherever you have your party.

will give the idea for separate rooms which will be visited on the journey through Wonder-Wander Land. If only one large room is available, the different corners can represent the different stages of the journey. All the lights should be carefully shaded and may peer forth from the eyes of crepe paper and wire heads of Buddahs, dragons and the like.

A huge dragon make of paper and wire with electrically lighted eyes may crouch in a dark corner and there may be a great number of paper snakes concealed in unexpected places and spiders with long wire legs dangling from the ceiling.

The Forest of Ancient Woe may be merely a particularly dark place where strange and unearthly noises are heard and where the Spirits have great difficulty in finding their way about. In one place they may struggle through a marsh—made of piles of crumpled newspaper; in another they will bump against strange and terrible "slimy things," which may be none other than our old friends, the raw oyster, the cold boiled spaghetti and the ice-filled rubber glove.

In the next place to which the Ghostly Guide will lead the Kindred Spirits will appear the Dwarf Behind the Twisted Pear Tree. The Twisted Pear Tree will be just as grotesque as pasteboard and paint can make it, and behind it will appear a huge Spider-Web of string which covers almost all of a corner of the room. Some huge imitation spiders will be seen caught in the web and there will be space enough at one side to admit any luckless Spirits who may be caught by the wicked Dwarf. The Dwarf, one of the smaller members of the Social Committee, will wear the queerest costume he can devise and a very ugly "false face." He will carry a net large enough to go over a person's head.

At the Tower of Apes, there will be a member of the Committee wearing a monkey "false face" or a head made according to the directions given on page 11.

From the Tower of Snakes another member may stretch out a long arm covered to represent a serpent.

In the corner of the room farthest from the door, a large figure of Buddha should be placed. This may be merely a realistic drawing. In the forehead of the Buddha should be the Ruby Wishing Stone, which may be made by inserting a small electric light covered with red paper, or merely by using red paint. Beneath the Buddha print the verse:

"Anyone who wanted things
 Touched the jewel and they came:
We were happier than kings
 If we could but do the same."

Program

The features of the program can be mentioned by the name in order to advertise the party, and the complete program can be printed upon a scroll hung from the mouth of a poster-dragon at the place where the guests are expected to first assemble. A great deal of interest will be aroused and there will be much conversation in the effort to guess what the journey really includes.

A NIGHT IN WONDER-WANDER LAND

PERSONALLY CONDUCTED BY THE GHOST OF AN OGRE

The Forest of Ancient Woe.
The Place of the Twisted Pear Tree.
The Tower of Apes.
The Tower of Snakes.
The Hall of the Ruby Wishing Stone.
Can Spirits Be Recognized?
Offerings to a God.
Commands of Buddha.
Who Am I?
Death Drill.
The Awful Fate of a Fibber.
The Flower of Old Japan.
The Ghost in the Well.

Carrying Out the Program

Experience has taught us that while the average young person likes the fun of a costume party, he is not particularly enthusiastic about spending an entire evening in clothes which are unfamiliar and uncomfortable. There are times, too, when it is impossible for some members of the group to prepare an elaborate costume, but anyone can borrow the sheet and pillow-case necessary for a ghost costume and since most ghost parties are planned so that the costume is removed as soon as the guests are identified the larger part of the evening can be spent in entire comfort. With this thought in mind, I have carefully planned our Night in Wonder-Wander Land which will, I am perfectly certain, furnish all the thrills that anyone could desire.

Much will depend upon the decorations which, without being expensive, will give an altogether different atmosphere to a well-known place. The Ghostly Guide, too, will have a large measure of responsibility. Upon his imagination and power of expression will depend a great deal of the spirit of the occasion.

As the guests assemble they may be taken in small groups through the different rooms which mark the stages of the journey and, if this is done, some assistant guides will be necessary. If only one room is to be used, the Guide should wait until the entire Ghostly Party is assembled.

When the Ghosts have passed through the Forest of Ancient Woe they will reach the Place of the Twisted Pear Tree and woe betide them there if they fail to escape from the clutches of the dwarf! A ring will be formed in the center of which is placed a chosen victim. If the Dwarf can catch the victim before the Ghosts in the ring have slowly chanted from one to ten, the victim will be placed in the Spider-Web, there to remain until time to play "Can Spirits be Recognized?"

The chances are largely in favor of the one whom the Dwarf hopes to catch in his net as the Dwarf himself is blindfolded.

At the Tower of Apes the Ghosts will attempt, blindfolded, to feed nuts to the Ape in charge. Those who fail will be given the mark of the Ape, a small penciled "A" upon their hand, which places them under a bewitchment to be removed only upon the performance of certain rites to be announced later.

At the Tower of Snakes those who fail, while blindfolded, to feed the Snake with a Sacred Honey Cake will be bewitched with the Mark of the Snake, a small circle representing a snake-bite and even more disastrous in its consequences than the Mark of the Ape.

At the Hall of the Ruby Wishing Stone the Spirits will be blindfolded and given the opportunity to go forward and kiss the Ruby Wishing Stone. Since the Wishing Stone is placed so high that even a tall Ghost will be obliged to rise on tip-toe, the performance will be decidedly amusing.

Can Spirits Be Recognized? All the Ghosts will form a circle with one Ghost in the center. The circle moves until the center Ghost cries "Stop!" and points to one of the Ghosts, who must then imitate a designated animal. If the center Ghost can recognize the voice, the other Ghost must unmask and become the center Ghost. If the center Ghost fails to guess correctly the circle must move again and he must keep on trying until he does succeed. This is a jolly game in itself as well as an effective way of unmasking.

Offerings to a God. Two or more teams, with a moon on a stick, a small table, a low dais, flowers, beans and chestnuts form in line shoulder to shoulder. At a given signal the first player of each team places the moon at a spot several yards distant: the second player places the table in front of the moon: the third player places the dais on the table and so on until all the flowers, etc., have been laid on the dais as an offering to the god. The team that has all the articles placed first, wins.

Commands of Buddha. About ten players are chosen and lined up at a starting place. A short distance from the start are placed ten mysteriously sealed envelopes which contain various instructions such as "Sing Yankee Doodle backward," "Give ten setting-up exercises," "Shake the hands of all the blue-eyed girls," "Imitate a man hunting his collar button," etc. All objects necessary for the carrying out of the directions are placed a short distance farther on the track. The players line up and at the signal run, pick up the envelopes, carry out directions and run to a fixed goal. The first to reach the goal, after having completed the assigned task, wins. Care must be taken that the stunts chosen will require about the same length of time.

Message from the Dead. Players form in two

lines shoulder to shoulder. "Starter" whispers a message to first player in each line. At a signal the message is whispered to the next player. The side that transmits the message correctly first, wins.

Who Am I? Names of famous people, names of other guests, names of occupations and the like are pinned on the backs of the players, two at a time occupying the center of the circle. Each must guess what he represents by the antics, impersonations or pantomimes of the other. In the case of names of famous people, questions to be answered by "Yes" and "No" may be asked.

Death Drill. Circle Game (seated). In Japanese the words *four* and *seven* contain characters meaning death. In this game the players count from one to seven, and from one to seven again, and so on around the circle, substituting for the words *four* and *seven* certain motions. For *four* pass the hand, palm up, under the chin toward the nose. For *seven* pass the hand around the head, from the chin, to the right, around the left to the chin again and up toward the nose. Those who make mistakes may give forfeits or leave the circle.

The Awful Fate of a Fibber (Part One—Chapter IX) should be performed by a small group prepared in advance.

At the conclusion of the stunt sembei (rice cakes) or kasuteria (sponge cake) and Goblin O cha (fruit punch) can be served, during which time selections from "The Flower of Old Japan" can be read. After this those marked with the mark of the Ape and the Snake will be called upon to perform stunts.

The Ghost in the Well. A true Japanese story, will then be related and the Kindred Spirits will be dismissed to the world of mortals again.

THE GHOST IN THE WELL

FROM THE STORY OF THE HAUNTED WELL
BY TOKICHI ISHII, "A GENTLEMAN IN PRISON"

Beyond the shadow of a doubt by the Temple of Yakushiji was haunted. Precisely at midnight every night groans so terrible that they must have startled even the dead in the nearby graveyard were heard to issue forth from the well. It was a place of dreadful terror and after nightfall the bravest man would not dare venture near it.

One day in broad daylight a number of people gathered there and peeped in, but the well was so deep and dark that they could not see the bottom. They lit a lantern and let it down, but even then they could see nothing. The well had not been used for a long, long time and there was rubbish up to the water-line.

Then said one of the men, "The god of the well has been insulted and his curse rests upon it. Let us ask the temple priests to pray that the curse be removed and let us meet each day at the well for counsel. So it may be that the curse will be removed."

So every day at noon the people assembled solemnly at the well and every day at sunrise and sunset the temple priests prayed long prayers, but every night at midnight the groaning went on as usual, until the hearts of the people of the neighborhood were stiff with terror.

Came a day when a little child said to his companion, "Let us go and look at the haunted well."

So they went—with boyish eagerness to look at the frightful object—and peeped in. As they leaned over the railing surrounding the well, it suddenly gave way and one of the lads, Yasujiro by name, tumbled in. His companion shrieked with fear and a great crowd came running to the spot, but no one made the slightest effort to rescue Yasujiro, for who would dare to descend the well that was haunted by the angry god?

Suddenly someone rushed off to tell the boy's father, and he came at once and in spite of his fear fixed a ladder long enough to reach to the bottom, let it down and descended with a lantern in his hand. The crowd waited breathlessly, and in a few moments the man reappeared with the fainting child in his arms. No serious harm had befallen either of them.

The people then inquired if there were not something unusual about the appearance of the well and the father went down a second time to investigate. He went down trembling with dread this time. Before, he had been too eager to save his son to consider consequences to himself: perhaps he supposed the god had let them go unharmed so as to tempt him into greater danger——

On a ledge far, far down in the well, he found . . . a black cat, all skin and bone and more dead than alive. The poor cat had fallen into the well and its cries of hunger and terror had been the dread sounds which were falsely attributed to the god of the well.

V

THE FESTIVAL OF NO-RUZ

A Persian Party

V

THE FESTIVAL OF NO-RUZ
A PERSIAN PARTY

A PARTY WITH TWO NAMES

A party with a name suggestive of an original program is always more appealing to young people than a "social," so two names are suggested for the Persian party. The name, "The Festival of No-Ruz" can be used accurately only in the Spring, as in Persia this festival celebrates the coming of Spring. However, the same plans may be used under the title, "A Visit to the Land of the Lion and the Sun." Sufficient program suggestions to admit of a wide variety of choice are given here. The party may be held indoors, with the decorative scheme as suggested, or it can be adapted delightfully to the requirements of a garden party.

Invitations

Poster invitations may be decorated with a sketch of the lion and the sun, or by birds and flowers, especially the nightingale and the narcissus. For example a poster with a narcissus and leaves at each side and a bird flying across the top might bear this invitation, suggested by the Persian poem, the "Rubaiyat":

"When the Bird of Time
Flies to March twenty-third
There will be joy for you
At the Festival of No-Ruz."

Another poster might be deep blue, with the pillared entrance to a Persian garden drawn in gold. The poster should be curved at the top and the picture almost cover the poster. Toward the top of the entrance gold stars should appear and the invitation should be printed below the stars in letters of black touched with gold.

Individual invitations may be decorated with birds or flowers or may be cut and folded in the shape of a tall gate with curving top, which opens at the center to disclose the invitation. Or they may be cut in the shape of birds or flowers or of the good-luck eggs which are plentiful at festival time. If egg-shaped, the invitations should be red.

Decorations

A Persian party will be a joyous challenge to the imaginative decorator. Without much expense beautiful effects can be arranged to create a true Persian atmosphere. An ugly basement room with supporting pillars quickly becomes the court of a Persian palace with the pillars covered with deep blue paper and arches of light wood covered with scarlet fastened between them.

Panels of blue studded with gold stars may decorate the walls, alternating with panels which bear, in gold lettering, famous Persian proverbs and verses.

There should be rugs and cushions or divans (these may be ordinary cots with bright covers and piled high with colored cushions). Bowls of gold-fish for good luck should stand on little tables or metal stands, and at one corner a stand may bear a tray of lucky eggs—dyed red, of course. Above them should appear this Persian prayer on a poster:

"O the Turner of the hearts and eyes,
O the Lord of night and day,
O the changer of conditions and dispositions,
Turn Thou our condition and better it."

The narcissus is especially typical of the Festival of No-Ruz but for decorations at the Persian party roses, lilacs, pinks and marigolds may also be used.

Dishes of candy should be placed in the doorway through which the guests enter and the members of the social committee who are receiving the guests will explain that this indicates a sweet and pleasant welcome.

The members of the social committee should, if possible, wear Persian costumes.

The man's costume consists of cotton trousers, gathered at the ankle, and blue shirt. A striped coat with long sleeves reaches to the knees and is fastened around the waist with a white cloth belt. A skull cap, over which a cloth is wrapped in turban style, forms the head-dress. (A kimono pattern can be used for the coat.)

The woman's costume is very gay. Her trousers are wide and full and gathered at the ankle. A chemise-like slip is worn over the trousers, hanging to the knees. Her head-dress is a square of muslin bound over the head with a cord or narrow strip of cloth. She wears a short veil fastened below the eyes and a long sheet of blue or white over her head and covering almost her entire costume.

Unbleached muslin and cheesecloth, dyed with Tintex, will make satisfactory and picturesque costumes.

Persian Proverbs for Decorative Posters

"When the lion appears, the jackal is silent."

"Sons of Adam from learning will find perfection
Not from dignity and rank and wealth and property."

"Like a taper one must melt in pursuit of learning
Since without learning one cannot know God."

"Deem every day in thy life as a leaf in thy history;
Be careful, therefore, that nothing be written in it unworthy of posterity."

"Sit not sad because that Time
A fitful aspect weareth,

Patience is most bitter, yet
Most sweet the fruit it beareth."
"Count not thy friend one who in fortune's hour
Boasts of his friendship and fraternity.
Him I call friend who sums up all his power
To aid thee in distress and misery."

Refreshments

Refreshments may be as simple or elaborate as desired. Food is served upon trays.

Typical Persian refreshments suitable for our party would be:

Sherbet-Fruit punch, quite sweet.

Cakes—Little flat cakes flavored with nuts, especially pistachio nits, cardamom, or caraway seeds.

Fruit-Grapes, peaches (called "Persian apples"), figs, apricots.

Nuts—Sugared burnt almonds, chestnuts.

Candy-Fruit paste or jelly (may be bought or made from recipe in book accompanying packages of Knox's gelatine); khulva—molasses nut taffy; pishmak—crystalized butter and sugar formed into odd shapes. (Try making butterscotch and dropping it by the spoonful into cold water.)

Program Suggestions

As the guests arrive, each one is announced in a loud voice by one of the members of the social committee. While the group is gathering the early arrivals may be entertained by a trained lion and dancing monkey. (See directions for making animal heads on page 11.)

The tricks of the lion may be as varied as the imagination of his trainer. The monkeys should dance with stiff, jerky steps, to the music of a tambourine (real or imitation).

When the entire group has gathered, each guest should receive a card bearing the name of an animal or bird, vegetable or fruit, flower or mineral found in Persia, and four groups should be formed. The group leader should ask each member to read his card, saying, "I am a lion," or "I am a peach," as the case may be. This will be funny and at the same time acquaint the young people with some of the native products of Persia.

Animals and Birds

Lion	Buffalo	Vulture
Tiger	Fat-Tailed Sheep	Blue Jay
Wolf	One-Humped Camel	Thrush
Leopard	Pigeon	Nightingale
Wild Cat	Eagle	Pelican
Fox	Hawk	Swan
Jackal		Stork
Wild Bear		

Vegetables and Fruits

Apple	Lemon	Caraway
Apricot	Spinach	Gherkins
Fig	Asparagus	Cherries
Citron	Rice	Plums
Orange	Wheat	Pears

MINERALS

Iron	Sapphire	Manganese
Lead	Carnelian	Gold
Silver	Copper	Borax
Topaz	Coal	
Emerald	Petroleum	

FLOWERS AND TREES

Narcissus	Four O'clock	Weeping Willow
Rose	Marigold	
Lilac	Pink	Acacia
Jasmins		

It may be necessary to use the same name more than once to keep the groups even. This, of course, will depend upon the number of guests.

After this each guest should be given a piece of muslin, some cotton batting, a pencil and thread and asked to construct a rag doll. (Persian children make their own dolls.) Or, if desired, the custom may be Americanized to the extent of providing lollipops, white paper for faces, pencils and crepe paper for the making of the dolls. Each group will display its dolls after the appointed time has passed and the maker of the most attractive doll will be rewarded with a book about Persia.

Following the doll making each group should appoint two representatives. These representatives will race over a given course on one leg, with the other tucked up stork-fashion. The stork is very highly honored in Persia and should appear on our program.

For another event each group may be represented in a ball-winding contest. (Persian children make their own balls.) Then yarn or string may be provided and the contest consist of seeing who can most swiftly wind a compact ball.

In the top-spinning contest each group may be represented by one or more of the boys. This event will be a real test of the skill of American boys.

According to the Persian custom all the tops are given to one player who tosses them into the air. One that does not fall on its flat surface is selected as a target and set spinning. The other players then wind their tops and hurl them over a distance of five or six feet at the top on the ground.

Persian Polo is an adaptation of a popular Persian custom. Courses are marked on the ground with chalk or tape and a blown egg—painted red, of course—placed at the beginning of each course. Each player representing a group is mounted upon a horse—a long stick with a carved wooden (or paper) horse's head—and armed with a fan. The object is to ride one's horse along the course, blowing the egg before one with the fan. If the egg is blown out of the boundary lines of the course, which should be very narrow, the rider must place the egg back at the beginning of the course.

The Persian stunt play, "The Bored King and the Bandit" will make a delightful dramatic feature for this part of the program. Following the stunt play refreshments should be served and during the refreshment period and perhaps afterwards the guests may engage in typical Persian after-dinner conversation. The first topic for discussion should be the amount eaten by other guests, a topic which is perfectly good form in Persia. The second topic should be some improbable question, but the discussion should be conducted in absolute seriousness. The social committee may select discussions which are local in their interest. Typical Persian themes are: "What would happen if the Caspian Sea should turn into a desert?" and "What would happen if the people had wings?" Especially brilliant conversationalists should be praised by the Persian compliment, "Plato in comparison with you is but as a dog."

Since chess and checkers are very popular in Persia, a chess or checker tournament would be an appropriate feature of a Persian party.

The departing guests are sped with these words: "May your shadow never grow less."

VI

MRS. SANTA CLAUS' RECEPTION

VI

MRS. SANTA CLAUS' RECEPTION

Here is a party plan which grew—as all good party plans must grow, out of imagination. It takes a basic idea, that of the farewell party by Mrs. Santa Claus to the toys and dolls made by Santa Claus and ready to go out to the boys and girls for Christmas. It uses the form of some familiar games, adapting them to this idea, and invents new games. It can be used for children, will be even more appreciated by the young people and will be hilarious for adults. While designed for Christmas, it has been gloriously successful at a Summer Camp in August.

Invitations

On long sheets of paper—cream colored is suggested—write or type the following jingle. Decorate the sheet with Santa Claus stickers and use a sticker to fasten it when folded.

Out of the shop of Santa Claus
  Go all the dolls and toys
Welcomed all over the world, because
  They are bringers of Christmas joys.
But don't you think that the Christmas toys
  Themselves should have some fun

Ere their task of pleasing the girls and boys
Is at Christmas-time begun?

Mrs. Santa Claus thinks so too
So she sends this message inviting you
To the Santa Claus Shop, where in formal state
The Toys Reception begins at eight.
Bring a ten-cent toy with you——
And don't be late!
Place ——————————
Date ——————————

The social room should be a gay reproduction of what you might imagine the shop of Santa Claus to look like. Over the entrance have a sign——

CHRISTMAS TOY SHOP
LATEST MODELS—DOLLS AND TOYS
S. CLAUS—PROPRIETOR

Decorate the walls with huge poster pictures of toys, in bright colors, red predominating. The pictures may be sketched roughly or made by cutting a toy out of colored paper and pasting it on a contrastingly colored poster. Small toys can be fastened on posters, so can ginger cookie men, animal crackers, etc. Have an empty table or two to hold the toys brought by the guests, which will be temporarily part of the decoration and then sent to an orphanage, hospital or other place where toys are needed. Small Christmas trees can be hung with candy toys and candy canes. An exhibit of dolls, loaned by the young women in the group, would be interesting. (Collecting dolls from different countries is, by the way, a fascinating hobby. I know! It's *my* hobby.) Paper dolls can be used effectively for decoration.

Refreshments can be served from a Noah's Ark built of compoboard or even constructed of sheets hung over wire with colored roof and windows of paper pinned on.

Mrs. Santa Claus should be a chubby person (her costume will make her so, if Nature hasn't) in bright red muslin dress with a white apron, white hair and cap and spectacles. Her assistants, the members of the social committee, should be dressed as workmen in overalls or smocks. Mr. Santa Claus will wear the usual costume but will not appear at the beginning of the program.

Refreshments should be colored fruit punch (use grape juice for color or the pure vegetable coloring sold by reliable grocers), gingerbread men, animal crackers, candy toys and canes, or lollipops and stick candy if the party is out of season.

Program

1. March of the Toys.
2. Engine Relay.
3. The Doll Shop.
4. Top Twirl.
5. Drawing Contest.
6. Story Book Show.
7. Parade of the Wooden Soldiers.

8. Jumping Jacks.
9. Feeding the Pets.

March of the Toys

After Mrs. Santa Claus has welcomed the guests they will be allowed about ten minutes to turn themselves into toys. For this purpose they may draw two articles from a table of supplies on which will be provided strips of colored crepe paper (for hair-ribbons for dolls or neckties for clowns), string (you might be a top and wind yourself up), old keys (so that you can be a mechanical toy), whistles (if you prefer to be a steam engine), old roller skate wheels, etc. Each player may use two articles to indicate what he represents but no more than two. When the toys are ready a lively march will be played and all the toys will march past Mr. Santa Claus who has by this time made a stately entrance driving his reindeer. He will award a toy prize to the best representation and put the least clever through some stunts. He may, for instance, suggest that they need more glue and have them try to feed each other (blindfolded) soft molasses taffies.

If preferred the guests may come to the party dressed as dolls or wooden soldiers. This plan makes a much jollier and more colorful party and the young people of the two camps where I tried it out loved the idea. They turned themselves into the most amazing dolls with only the contents of a camper's suitcase to help them.

Engine Race

The difficulty with mechanical toys is that they are apt to be balky when wound up. The engine race is a relay, with the entire group divided into four teams. They line up at one end of the room and the first player in each line starts at the signal toward a mark at the other end of the room. All the while he goes he must make a noise suggesting some kind of engine, the "chug-chug" of a locomotive, the Clang! Clang! of a fire-engine, etc. And instead of racing directly forward he must go forward six steps, then back two, two to right, then two to left, repeating the process to the goal and back to the line where he touches off the next player who will proceed in the same way. The first line to have every player back in place wins.

The Doll Shop

While the Engine Relay is going on have about ten of the guests preparing the next stunt—"The Doll Shop"—during which Santa will be salesman and one of the players the customer. Each of the others will represent a different kind of doll—a walking doll, jigging doll, talking doll, baby doll, even a broken doll could be included. Santa will show the customer each doll, and the customer will find fault with each until at last one pleases him and he goes off with it under his arm.

Top Twirl

Divide the entire company into groups of two, each player being either the Top or the String with the exception of about six or more players who are Strings whose Tops have been lost. Top and String will clasp right hands facing each other. At the first whistle of the leader String will run around Top, turing Top as he runs. At the second whistle String stands still while Top twirls around, at the third whistle Tops suddenly stop and hold up their right hands while each String rushes to get a new Top. Some Strings, will, of course, be left and will wait until the next time to try to catch a Top. No String may have the same Top twice. This will be especially good fun if a rollicking tune is played on the piano and the Tops hum the tune while spinning.

Drawing Contest

Four lines of about eight each are lined up facing a blackboard (or four large posters) as far away as the size of the room permits. At the starter's signal the first person in each line runs forward and draws the head of Santa Claus, who is posing for his portrait. After drawing the artist hurries back to give his chalk or crayon to the next member of his team who puts in Santa Claus's features. The next player adds his neck, the next his body, the next his arms, the next his feet, the last the finishing touches. The winning team must be judged for the artistic effect of the portrait as well as the speed with which it was completed.

Story Book Show

Divide the entire party into groups of from six to ten and give each group a turn at acting out a familiar children's story in pantomime. This may be done directly in front of the audience or behind a sheet with the audience in darkness and a light back of the players. The Proud Princess—(Part One, Chapter V) will be very appropriate to use here.

Parade of the Wooden Soldiers

The entire company will line up in single file and march stiffly and with jerky steps and absolutely solemn faces past Santa Claus, while the "Parade of the Wooden Soldiers" is played slowly. Santa by making faces or remarks will endeavor to make the soldiers laugh as they pass and repass him. Each soldier who laughs must leave the line. The last to remain in line should be awarded a black crepe band for his arm—high honor in the Legion of Wooden Heads!

Jumping Jacks

A race for four to ten players, each player proceeding from start to goal with the following movement—hands on hips, deep knee bend, jump forward. Straighten up, deep knee bend, jump forward.

Feeding the Pets

Refreshment-time, accompanied by Christmas stories, such as The Coming of the Prince, Eugene Field; A Christmas Present for a Lady, (In Little Citizens), Myra Kelly; Christmas, Zona Gale; Gifts of the Magi, O. Henry, and The Doll That Saved a War (in "Peace Crusaders"), by Griscom.

Christmas songs can be used or selections such as "I Can't Do That Sum" from Victor Herbert's "Babes in Toyland."

HETERICK MEMORIAL LIBRARY
793.24 B194s
Balm, Catherine Atki/Stunts of all lands
onuu
3 5111 00103 5546